PSYCHIC ADVANTAGE:

Key to Controlling

People and Situations

Also by the Author

Miracle of Instant Memory Power,
Parker Publishing Co., Inc.

PSYCHIC ADVANTAGE:

Key to Controlling People and Situations

David V. Lewis

Parker Publishing Company, Inc. · West Nyack, N.Y.

Library of Congress Cataloging in Publication Data

Lewis, Dave.
  Psychic advantage.

  Includes index.
  1. Control (Psychology) 2. Success. I. Title.
BF632.5.L48   158   79-14864
ISBN 0-13-732032-9

Printed in the United States of America

This book is dedicated to:
Leta, Lyn and Lisa

How This Book Can Help You

This book will show you how to use a powerful force called *psychic advantage* to greatly increase your position in *all* your dealings with others.

What is *psychic advantage?* Above all, it is a dynamic mental force — a state of mind — possessed by those who always seem to be in complete control.

It is this dynamic mental force, coupled with proven tactics and techniques discussed in this book, that will give you tremendous new leverage in dealing with people and situations.

Perhaps you, like me, have been confused by the "patterns of success" you see in everyday life. People no smarter than you are getting promotions. People no more talented than you are making bigger names. People no more dedicated than you are making far more money. Why?

After years of observation and analysis, the answer has come into full focus. These people have somehow learned to gain the mental upper hand — *psychic advantage* if you will — in their daily relations with others.

The beauty of it is, psychic advantage is a state of mind that can be acquired by anyone who will take the time and effort to master the simple but proven techniques discussed in this book.

To begin with, those who have psychic advantage know and understand the nature of true *power.* They realize intuitively how to use power to gain leverage when dealing with others, below or *above* them in station.

Once you understand the nature of true power, you'll be able to use the latent powers that have existed within you for years. You'll exude a mystique of power that will help you gain a clear *psychic advantage* over others. You'll also learn how to cope with power when you're the underdog, as we all are at one time or another.

This type of power leverage, for example, coupled with a working knowledge of sound strategies, enabled John Livingston, a purchasing agent, to negotiate contracts and issues with more confidence and expertise — and success — than he had ever had before.

He learned how to use *association* — and *disassociation* — to advantage and how to use tactics such as *limited authority, fait accompli, statistics,* and *brinksmanship,* among others, to gain a clear-cut edge in dealing with others.

While possessing *psychic advantage* does put you in a dominant position with friends and associates, it doesn't preclude the use of diplomacy in gaining the upper hand. In fact, being able to detect and satisfy human needs is an integral part of achieving *psychic advantage.* You can enhance your own position by elevating the other person's self-esteem or giving him a chance to use his own talents to greater advantage.

People who hold *psychic advantage* are almost always master communicators. Thus, we'll take pains to sharpen the skills required in this field.

For example, Jane Baker was a file clerk until she learned how to "talk." Now, using the techniques discussed in this book, she can dominate any conversation without appearing to do so. She consistently wins in the daily "war of words." She has, in fact, talked her way into an executive position in her company.

Efficient listening is certainly another valuable skill you'll want to sharpen. By listening selectively "between the lines" and by learning to idle your mental motor, you'll acquire new confidence in your ability to deal with others.

There's also the matter of learning how to code and decode the many nonverbal messages that you are bombarded with daily and how to send your own messages to gain *psychic advantage.*

You'll also learn to master one other key communications skill, one that is frequently overlooked — the ability to ask probing, productive questions. Jim Blackburn did and soon found himself a member of the Million Dollar Club.

Jim discovered, as you will in this book, how to use key questions to sustain an interview; how to pose leading, even loaded, questions that kept him in a dominant position; and how to ask questions that will close a deal.

And finally, you'll learn how to tap the latent creativity within you. This will give you fresh, innovative ways to cope with people and problems.

Psychic advantage is easy to learn and easy to apply — once you make the commitment to use the dynamic mental force that has always been a natural part of your makeup. The application of psychic advantage is so low-key, so subtle, that others will not know you are using it. Yet you will be able to recognize when others are using it on you, and you will be able to neutralize it or counter with your own winning tactics.

Psychic advantage will almost certainly make your life happier and more productive.

By controlling others, you can more successfully contend with the complex people problems and situations that you are confronted with daily...thanks to *psychic advantage.*

David V. Lewis

Contents

Developing the Mystique of Power Through Psychic Advantage *(cont.)*

PSYCHIC ADVANTAGE:

Key to Controlling
People and Situations

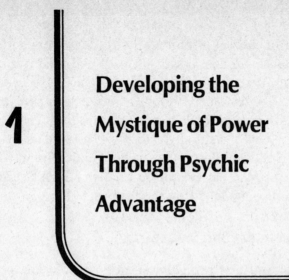

Developing the Mystique of Power Through Psychic Advantage

Three years ago, Mel Forster was about to abandon his career as a salesman. Today, he's one of the top producers in his company.

What turned things around for Mel? "It's simple," he points out. "I just learned how to gain the 'upper hand' in most of my dealings with other people."

"Upper hand" means *psychic advantage* — the ability to control people and situations a good part of the time.

A universal truth

Psychic advantage is based on a universal truth: In virtually every relationship between two people, one usually assumes superiority, however slight, for one reason or another. Only rarely will both parties to a transaction consider themselves really equal.

The *reasons* people use to assume superiority constitute

the rationale, or basis, of psychic advantage. Appearance, dress, personality, position, age, power — these and a host of other conditions are used as a basis for assuming leverage over another person. You can improve your ability to gain psychic advantage by better understanding and exploiting these conditions.

Some people, naturally, come by psychic advantage more easily. Still, experience shows that almost anyone who is willing to work at it can acquire a relatively high degree of psychic advantage by following three steps.

Three steps to psychic advantage

First, be *aware* that in almost every relationship, people are striving for dominance, or psychic advantage, whether they realize it or not.

Second, observe *how* some people consistently gain psychic advantage in their relations with others.

Third, master the techniques and strategies employed by those who do maintain a high degree of psychic advantage a good deal of the time.

How Mel Forster gained advantage

For example, Mel was able to pinpoint his problem as one of credibility. "For whatever reason," he said, "prospects didn't seem to place a great deal of faith in what I told them. I would quote all the 'right' sources and say what the company considered to be the 'right' things. But somehow, I just didn't seem to instill trust, which is fatal in a sales situation."

So what do you do when you're not successful? It's simple: You look at someone who is. That someone was Bill Blackmon, the company's top producer, who obviously *was* believable. Mel began to study his style to see what made him tick.

"Show and tell"

"After a dozen calls with Bill, I began to get the picture," Mel said. "Clients believed Bill because he not only *told* them how good he and his product were, he *showed* them.

"Bill worked letters from satisfied customers into his presentation. These included letters from well-known citizens and even prominent sports figures in the community. He managed to do this so professionally and unobtrusively that there was not even the slightest hint of immodesty in his pitch.

"It may sound corny," Mel continued, "but all I know is that I started using the same approach and my sales shot up by about 30 percent in less than a year."

Why does the testimonial technique give Mel psychic advantage? For the same reason the principle works so well for most major corporations that have famous people endorse their products. It's a phenomenon called *transference*. People tend to transfer the quality a person possesses in one field to another field, even though the latter might be totally unrelated.

The public's thinking becomes: If it's good enough for somebody who's famous, it's good enough for me.

The benefits to be gained

This is the way Mel discovered and began to gain psychic advantage through the *mystique of power.*

Once you develop this mystique yourself, you can improve your ability to gain psychic advantage greatly. You stand a good chance to:

- Revitalize your self-image.
- Control people and situations to a far greater degree.
- Grow into a position of leadership.

- Influence others more readily.
- Develop a personality that attracts and demands attention from others.

Following are some of the primary ways to develop psychic advantage through the mystique of power.

Gaining psychic advantage through knowledge

Knowledge is power. Sure, you've heard the expression a million times before. But are you using this basic truth to full advantage? If not, you're missing out on one sure-fire way of gaining psychic advantage.

People in "power professions" — notably doctors, lawyers, top accountants and other executives — routinely hold psychic advantage in their relations with others.

Controlling health and wealth

The reason is rather obvious. These people have mastered a highly specialized area of knowledge. It is this knowledge that gives them a high degree of "control" over two of your most coveted possessions: health and wealth.

On a professional basis, this power is almost absolute. In other areas of life, it is almost as great. Here again, transference is at work. If a person is adept at performing an appendectomy or advising you about an intricate tax matter, he or she is equally proficient at telling you how to run your marriage or a small business. Or at least that's a conclusion most of us are willing to reach.

Doing your own thing

So what happens if you're not a doctor or lawyer? How, then, can you develop the knowledge mystique of power?

It's simple, really. All you have to do is to acquire an extensive body of knowledge within your own business, profession, or "specialty."

Linda Clarke discovered this basic truth and used it to leap-frog her way from a clerical to a professional position in her company, a major home-construction firm.

As a clerk, Linda did lots of "paper-shuffling" for executives, using only a fraction of her capabilities.

How Linda asserts herself

But Linda was ambitious, smart, and assertive. While shuffling paper, she noticed that the marketing department was basing its projections on future sales mainly on past performance.

"This didn't take into account economic conditions or the changing attitude of buyers, among other things," Linda said. "I knew there had to be a better way of projecting sales, so I started researching every single factor that impacted on home-buying — finance, population shifts, geographic distribution, and what have you.

"Within six months, I had amassed a wealth of material. Then I came up with a profile of what the future home buyer would look like.

"The next step was easy. I put the results of this research into a slick presentation and presented it to the marketing department. It really opened their eyes."

Virtually from that moment on, Linda became *the* authority on future home buyers. And since she was obviously more knowledgeable than anyone else on the subject, her promotion to manager became more or less automatic.

This is an era of specialization. The more knowledge you have and the more of an expert you become in any given area, the greater your chances of gaining clear psychic advantage.

Les Sebastian, sales representative for a national management consultant firm, used knowledge — or more appropriately, you might call it "research" — to gain his version of psychic advantage.

"As a new salesman, one of my biggest problems was getting on the same wave length with new customers," he said. "It was just hard for me to establish rapport."

Helping solve problems

"Then, quite by accident, I discovered what my problem was. I was trying to get some business from an especially hard-nosed vice president, and I thought to myself, 'Oh no, here we go again.' But before long things were going my way. This hard-nosed character and I were really communicating with each other, and I walked away with a substantial contract."

It didn't take Les long to analyze the reason for his success. He was extremely knowledgeable in the area of psychological testing, and as it happened, the potential customer's biggest problem at the moment was hiring and keeping the right kind of people.

Research is the key

Quite by accident, Les had uncovered the key to his future success: helping others solve *their* problems.

"That's it," Les confirms. "It's easy to talk with people — and yes, to *sell* them — if you can help them solve their problem. Since that time, I've never gone to a major appointment without first researching the company and people involved to find out what their problem might be. And significantly, I have never run into a company that does not have problems. They might think they don't have them, in which case it's my job to help them find out what they are."

Knowledge mystique is conveyed in still another form: legitimacy. For instance, we *assume* that anything with an "official seal" affixed or anything that appears to be "legal" is, indeed, the real McCoy.

How a diploma shows "legitimacy"

One real estate company offers a "special warranty" printed in Old English type on a parchment paper. The warranty really offers little more than the company's *word* that they will do what they say. But it apparently gives the public a sense of security when dealing with the firm.

Some businessmen gain a degree of psychic advantage by adorning their office walls with similar pieces of paper.

Gaining psychic advantage through information power

Almost as good a source of psychic advantage as knowledge is *information* about people and things. This includes scuttlebutt about what's going on — or better still, what's about to go on — in an organization or in people's private lives.

The rumor monger in industry, the gossipy housewife at the bridge club, the know-it-all neighbor — they all have something in common. They have worked very hard at becoming a solid source of information. The reward for such resourcefulness is that they have acquired the mystique of power.

Right or wrong, people gravitate toward these people in order to satisfy a basic need: to know and understand what's going on around them. This technique is especially powerful in a situation where poor communication exists, which is almost everywhere.

How Ed Maloney used information

Ed Maloney is a case in point. His rise from service-station mechanic to successful real estate operator was mainly a result of his "nose for news."

A curious and gregarious person by nature, Ed deals with people on a "personal basis." He not only finds out what's wrong with their car, but also shows a marked interest in their personal and business life.

In time, Ed naturally accumulated a wealth of information about his suburban community and the people in it. All of this paid off when one of Ed's favorite customers, a commercial Realtor, began to secretly option land in the area for a proposed shopping center. Before each transaction, the Realtor would consult Ed about how owners felt about their land and what kind of deal they expected.

How Ed got a new job

Sensing what an important role he was playing in the overall transaction, Ed accosted his Realtor friend one day. "Mr. Baker," he said, "I think I could do a great job for you, just like I'm doing on this deal. How about putting me on the payroll?"

The Realtor agreed, and within a year, Ed became a full-time partner in the enterprise. Indeed, *information* can be a valuable ally in your quest for psychic advantage through the mystique of power.

Gaining psychic advantage through the mystique of appearance

Good-looking people have power. People who are good-looking and, in addition, dress well have even more power.

People who are good-looking, dress well, and are extremely knowledgeable practically write their own ticket.

Ralph started a health program

Ralph Waggoner is like many who have attained a degree of psychic advantage by altering their physical appearance. At one point, he was 75 pounds overweight, a fact which affected his performance and his relations with associates.

"I often found myself running out of gas," he said. "And in this condition you can hardly impress others."

But all that changed after Ralph started a strict health regime, which included jogging and working out regularly with light weights at the health club.

How he gained control

Within a year, Ralph had pared off 50 pounds. He looked and acted like a much younger man. His appearance was further enhanced by a tan developed for the most part under a sun lamp.

How did all of this increase Ralph's psychic advantage? "All I know," he said, "is that a healthy appearance can make a big difference in how people react toward you. I feel that my new look has given me more control over myself — and others, too."

Plastic surgery the answer?

If appearance is power and does offer a high degree of psychic advantage, isn't it possible to gain psychic advantage through cosmetic surgery?

It is possible, and many people do just that. The number of plastic surgeons has increased dramatically in the United

States since World War II. One of these practitioners, the late Dr. Maxwell Maltz, became a nationally known figure through his best-selling book, *Psycho-Cybernetics.*

How an ad man gains confidence

In the book, Dr. Maltz reports many case histories of people who, once they had had a physical anomaly removed, improved their personality, job performance, and overall outlook on life. They improved their chances of gaining psychic advantage greatly.

I know firsthand of one such instance, an advertising man we'll call Art. Art was a sharp dresser and good-looking in a rugged sort of way. One relatively minor "flaw" in his physical makeup was a hook nose.

The problem was, Art didn't consider the flaw all that minor. And when he was elevated to vice president of his firm and started dealing with top executive clients, the flaw — to him — became major. Gaining psychic advantage under such circumstances was virtually impossible.

The operation "works"

Art had his nose straightened through surgery, and the change in his outlook was almost instant. He found himself more at ease with top executives and in time began to gain his fair share of psychic advantage in his relations with both clients and associates.

All such operations don't work out so happily. As Dr. Maltz points out in his book, fully half of the people he operated on did not change their outlook substantially.

Sometimes, in other words, the "scar" is psychic, locked deep down in the individual's subconscious. It takes more than an operation to modify behavior in these circumstances.

Gaining psychic advantage through the mystique of prestige

The president of almost any business or social organization usually has a relatively high degree of power.

In corporations, the sometimes frantic scramble to reach the top of the heap is as much for prestige as it is for the money. "Sure, money's important," one top-level executive said. "But after you reach a certain level — and I think most of my counterparts in industry feel the same way about this — why, money is just something to keep score by." What really becomes important is what the money stands for. After a while, you sort of lose track of what your actual take-home pay is, but you're increasingly aware of the continuing struggle for power in the organization.

Prestige pays off

Bradley Hamilton, who owns a large mortgage company, plays prestige power to the hilt by giving most of his employees who deal with the public a title such as "vice president."

"This definitely gives these people psychic advantage," he said. "Generally, the public would much rather deal with a vice president than with a plain-vanilla employee. And in truth, it doesn't cost me a penny more."

An individual can add to his own power position by using an imaginative title. For example, Gloria Riley, a public stenographer, figures she gains psychic advantage by billing herself as a "communications consultant." Sumner Thomas' job of adding home improvements doesn't sound too prestigious until he becomes an "innovations engineer."

Prestige is one of the more effective ways to achieve psychic advantage.

Gaining psychic advantage through the mystique of money power and politics

Political power goes hand in glove with money power. *Transference* is at work here again. People with money become instant experts in just about everything. Money talks, and when it does, almost everybody listens.

Politics at work

Being able to persuade others to your point of view through politics is a prime source of psychic advantage.

The late Lyndon B. Johnson, an unabashed expert at getting things done through others, was a prime example. Johnson came from a South Texas family of modest means. He virtually button-holed his way into the Senate, and ultimately, the Presidency.

But politics is not confined to the White House. It permeates the business and social world. And the person who becomes adept at it — the wheeler-dealer as he or she is sometimes called — gains true psychic advantage over most others.

How "power people" prevail

There are other ways to gain psychic advantage through the mystique of power. But they all seem to spring mainly from these sources. If you will observe carefully, you'll notice that the "power people" in your business and social spheres maintain a high degree of psychic advantage.

What if you don't measure up?

So what does all this mean? Obviously, it means that you can gain a great deal of psychic advantage by being rich, good-looking, and smart. But that eliminates many right off the bat. In addition, it obviously helps immeasurably to be a master politician, hold a prestigious position, and be highly regarded as an expert in one or more fields. But again, many fall by the wayside using these standards.

There are few such human paragons around. In fact, it's probably the exceptional individual who has clear superiority in any one of these power areas.

But there definitely are ways to improve your psychic advantage in each of these areas, and we'll be discussing these ways throughout the book. Naturally, your improvement will be in direct proportion to the effort you are willing to expend.

Improvement takes time

Still, there will be limitations, in many cases, to the improvement you can make in raising your psychic advantage level by exploiting your power positions. For example, a person of modest appearance (and doesn't this include most of us?) can make certain cosmetic improvements. But well-tailored clothes can often make an even bigger difference.

Becoming knowledgeable in a subject — an expert, if you will — normally takes some time. In other words, improving your position in any of the power areas is normally a continual process, requiring self-discipline.

Well, then, doesn't this paint a pretty bleak picture for those of us who now recognize that gaining psychic advantage through power mystique takes time, patience, and persistence — and especially for those of us who will only be able to make modest gains, regardless of the amount of work we put into it?

Not necessarily. You can improve more than you dream if you will take the time and trouble to master and use some additional and, in all probability, little-used principles of psychic advantage through power.

These principles are obvious to any discerning person. But they are fully exploited only by those who pursue the quest for psychic advantage through the mystique of power with gusto. They are:

- Psychic advantage must be recognized by others before it exists.
- It is possible to have psychic advantage with no advantage at all.
- Find out how much people will submit to, and you can establish your psychic advantage base.
- Psychic advantage positions constantly change, depending on the expectation level of the people involved.

Let's take a look at these ideas in action.

Psychic advantage must be recognized by others before it exists

Bradley Wright is an unassuming, rather mild-mannered auditor for a Texas-based conglomerate. He is average in both intelligence and appearance; in fact, he ranks low in most of the power categories, except for his accounting ability. This, however, is minimized somewhat by his relatively low position in the company.

Despite these "shortcomings," Bradley manages to frequently hold his own in negotiations with more powerful business associates. He does so mainly because he recognizes that psychic advantage does not really exist unless it is *recognized*.

How Wright prevails

For example, Bradley will stroll into the office of a top executive, let's say the vice president of manufacturing, and announce that he's about to make a quarterly audit. The conversation goes like this.

> **Vice President:** We're on a tight schedule here. I'd like for you to wrap this thing up by Tuesday noon at the latest.
> **Bradley:** Mr. Jones, I hope your people are complying with the new government directive PSG-2-3. It's been giving us a fit at some of the other divisions.
> **Vice President:** I think you'll find that we go by the book here. Should be no problem. Now, what do you think about that Tuesday deadline?
> **Bradley:** We'll see. And incidentally, we're going to have to go over your political donations with a fine-toothed comb this year after what happened at the corporate office last year.
> **Vice President:** Political donations, huh?...Well, we're all right there, I'm sure...but tell you what, better talk to me when you get into that part of it.
> **Bradley:** Fine. We'll be glad to. Now I guess we better get started. This is going to take some time.
> **Vice President:** I see. Well, fine. But don't forget to see me when you get to the political donations...."

How and why limited power pays off

Get the point! Bradley is using his very limited psychic advantage source — his accounting expertise and knowledge of the tax laws and company policy — along with the notion that advantage doesn't really exist if you don't fully recognize it in the first place. Bradley "ignored" the vice president's *demand* for a quick audit and played a power game by stressing potential danger spots that *he* knew about.

The idea is to minimize the more powerful party's elevated status by coupling your own limited power source with the truism that psychic advantage must be acknowledged to exist.

Jennifer Lowry is another case in point. She's a successful real estate operator today, but it wasn't always so.

"When I first started, they just said, 'Here's your desk and there's the phone. Go to it,'" she said.

How Jennie used limited psychic advantage

So how did Jennie manage to maintain some semblance of power in intricate real estate transactions with other brokers and many clients who knew more about real estate than she did? What did she do when they "exercised" this advantage by injecting legal jargon and technicalities into the transaction?

She did more or less what came naturally. She retaliated with her primary source of power — her looks and her graceful manner.

She prepared by clothing her attractive body with equally attractive and expensive clothing. Then she learned to say, with a wilting smile and disarming grace: "I don't know, but I'll certainly find out and get right back with you." Then she would pour it on personality-wise.

In effect, Jennie was "ignoring" the query, which was a ploy used by some clients to show their vast knowledge of real estate. It didn't take Jennie long to learn the game, and this led to her success.

The surprise element helps

Naturally, this tactic must be used with discretion. Common sense dictates to Jennie just how far to go with it.

What makes this move work so well in many cases is the surprise element. Most people in authority, or in a power position in a given situation, are accustomed to having people kowtow to them. When someone "questions" their authority, their reaction tends to be: "How can this person assume such a position in my presence? He *must* know something I don't know."

It sometimes works better with outside contacts, who haven't yet discovered that there's no real justification for your game; that you're bluffing.

It is possible to have psychic advantage with no advantage at all

In the foregoing cases, Bradley and Jennie fared quite well with *limited* authority. But what about the person who has virtually no advantage at all? Can he or she play the power game successfully? Paradoxically, he or she can, and we'll discuss *how* more thoroughly in the following chapters.

But to illustrate the point, let's look briefly at the classic case of the teen-ager (no advantage) confronted by his authoritarian father (all advantage). The conversation goes like this:

How "no advantage" wins out

Father: Now, Bobby, I've asked you nicely a dozen times or more to get your hair cut. Now I'm going to insist on it.

Bobby: But Dad, I like my hair the way it is.

Father: *You* might, but *I* don't.

Bobby: But all the other fellows wear their hair like mine.

Father: I don't care what the other fellows are doing. This is *my* house, and as long as you live here, what I say goes.

Bobby: Well, Dad, you're right. It is *your* house, and I'm gonna check it to you. I've been thinking about dropping out of school and getting a job anyway. A couple of fellows and myself will be getting our own apartment right away.

The father, who is dead set on Bobby eventually getting a law degree, is over a barrel. His psychic advantage has been usurped in one stroke — by a youngster who has *no* power at all.

This type of shenanigan is a little more difficult to pull off in the hurly-burly business world. But it *can* be done.

How a secretary gains stature

A long-time, dedicated secretary, for example, is often one of an executive's most prized "possessions." In many instances, she is literally an extension of the boss himself. She writes most of his letters, does some of his administrative work, protects him from the outer world, and literally runs the show during his absence (and sometimes when he's there).

Dorothy Hammond of Houston is such a prized secretary. And though she is not listed on the organizational chart, she manages to have her way when the chips are down.

In order to get major concessions such as special trips, long weekends, modern office furniture, and other favors, Dorothy now and then flat threatens to quit. She doesn't do it frequently, mind you, just often enough to keep her boss honest.

Making "threats" appear valid

But when she does pose the threat, it *appears* genuine enough. He'll complain mildly and then accede to her demands. Another case of no-advantage competing successfully with all-advantage and "winning!"

The key to success in using this tactic is to use it infrequently so as to make the threat seem real. Then, too, you must be prepared to follow through, or back down, just in case things don't work out. After all, no one in the organization is indispensable, not even Dorothy.

There are other subtle ways of making the threat *appear*

real, such as jotting down the name of a placement service on your memo pad or telling the boss about a friend of yours who just went to work for an oil company at "twice my salary." There *are* ways. Think about them.

Find out what people will submit to and you can establish your psychic advantage base

Master players of the psychic advantage game seem to have one major advantage over non-power participants. They're not only consistently seeking ways to gain psychic advantage, they have a habit of applying constant pressure to demonstrate and expand that advantage.

David G., president of a multi-division manufacturing firm, is such a power player, and it has apparently paid him enormous dividends. He joined the company as an administrative assistant five years ago and has leap-frogged his way up to president of operations for all divisions.

How David G. goes the limit

Mr. G. plays the game with subordinates and superiors alike. He uses roughly the same tactics on either group, modifying them only to fit the person and the situation.

Here's how he played the power game with Paula, his secretary. At first, he requested of her only the tasks that were included in her job description. Then came the "encroachments."

First, he asked her to bring him coffee (light cream, no sugar). When this worked, he requested that she bring coffee for committee meetings and conferences he was holding in his office. She reluctantly complied, complaining only to her associates that "I didn't hire on as a waitress."

The strategy of increasing demands

Having made these slight inroads, Mr. G. pressed on. A few weeks later, he asked Paula to pick up his lunch and bring it back to the office; the next week, it was a personal errand to another office building; the next it was to pick up his favorite tobacco and a suit that he had had altered.

Mr. G. was piling up "power points" galore. Then, one day, he found the limits of his power. "Paula," he said, "I'd like for you to drop by Macy's and pick out an anniversary present for my wife. I'm terribly busy today." Paula declined, and not altogether gracefully. By refusing, Paula was saying, "That's it, Mr. G. You've gone as far as you can go."

When to stop demands

That's true, but the point is: Look how far Mr. G. had gone. He had already established broad power parameters with Paula. Too, he was smart enough to realize that Paula was becoming a dedicated and proficient secretary, a fact that was swinging the balance of power more in her favor. In a moment, we'll discuss how power positions change as the degree of expectation changes within people.

While developing his power position with Paula, Mr. G. followed rather scrupulously his own ground rule of making power plays that could be both *seen* and *heard.* "After all," he said, "if no one *knows* you have psychic advantage, what good is it?" The obvious conclusion: The more *visible* power is, the greater it is.

Playing power games with superiors

Now, playing power games with your secretary is one thing. Playing them with your boss, who is likely to be somewhat of a power player himself, is another. Still, Mr. G. managed to do quite well with his superior, Sam.

When dealing with Sam, Mr. G. was careful to always "request" rather than "order," and he would always "justify" his action.

For example, Mr. G. called a meeting of the division's operating council — the decision-making body of the company — in his office one day. The strategy is obvious. It looks good for the company brass to be seen meeting in his office. It gives the appearance of the top powers meeting on Mr. G's "home ground," and at *his* request. Conclusion: Mr. G. must be on the way up.

When it's time to "volunteer"

Mr. G. "justified" holding the meeting in his bailiwick by "volunteering" to have his secretary, Paula, take minutes and pass them out that very day. (This was the result of an earlier power play he had made with Paula.)

Mr. G. made further points by having Sam speak to his service club ("They'd like to hear it from a real expert"), by having Sam officiate at his son's Little League playoff game ("It would mean so much to have a former college star officiating"), and by having Sam play in his golf foursome ("If you don't mind playing with a bunch of duffers"). The golf invitation led to other social incursions. To make all these things more *visible*, Mr. G. made certain that they somehow found their way into the company newspaper, or at the very least, the company bulletin board.

Psychic advantage positions often change, depending on the expectation level of the people involved

Psychic advantage is rarely constant. All-powerful politicians can become "one of the boys" in a single balloting. Executives can go up and down the hierarchy like yo-yos. And most notably, entertainment and sports celebrities, except those in the very highest super-star bracket, can become "unknowns" in a jiffy.

And so it is, to a lesser degree, in personal relationships, both business and social. One's power position can change, for one reason or another, from day to day, even from minute to minute.

Getting what you "expect"

Psychic advantage is inseparable from what psychologist Abraham Maslow calls aspiration level, which is nothing more than an *expected* result.

For instance, let's say we have two people applying for an executive position. One applicant has high hopes; he *expects* to get a high five-figure income and, as a result, asks for it. The other would *like* to have such an income, but subconsciously *expects* to get a salary in the lower five-figure category.

How the higher aspiration level wins

All things being equal, the person with the higher expectation level usually gets his or her way. This has been demonstrated at the negotiation table, where the party that expects more almost always ends up getting more.

The point of all this is that the person with the constantly high expectation level is almost certain to have a higher degree of psychic advantage in his relationships than the person who aspires to a lower degree of power.

The implication here is quite clear: Increase your expectation level, and you increase your ability to gain psychic advantage in your relationships with others.

But all this begs a question. Why does one person have a high expectation level and another a low one? And if your expectation level is low, is there a way you can raise it and in the process attain a higher degree of psychic advantage? The answer to these questions is critical to your being able to reach your goals, and it behooves you to master the techniques discussed in this book.

Now, the person who really understands psychic advantage realizes that your expectation level, thus your psychic advantage, can change even in the course of a conversation or in the middle of a negotiation.

Expectations can go down

If the executive seeking a very high salary gets a favorable indication from the interviewer, his aspiration level goes up. If he gets a frown or some other negative indicator, it tends to go down (unless, of course, he has an unshakably high aspiration level; something we'll strive for in our quest for psychic advantage).

He realizes — quite wisely — that the balance of power is shifting constantly. For example, you'll recall that Mr. G. was playing the power game to the hilt when he suddenly realized that he had gone as far as he could go with Paula. He perceived that the balance of power had, as a matter of fact, shifted rather suddenly, and he modified his behavior immediately.

It is this ability to shift with the tide that enables power people to maintain high psychic advantage in their relations with others.

KEY IDEAS

There are three basic steps you must take to achieve mastery in the realm of psychic advantage. They are:

1. Be *aware* of the people who have psychic advantage.

2. *Observe* these people in action.
3. Master the strategies and techniques that are successful.

You can develop the mystique of power by:

- Gaining credibility through the "testimonial technique."
- Using the psychology of *legitimacy*.
- Becoming a powerful source of information.
- Exploiting *appearance* to your advantage.
- Capitalizing on the benefits of money and politics.

Further expand your power base by exploiting these little-known, thus rarely used, principles of power:

1. Power must be recognized before it exists.
2. It is possible to have a power advantage even when you have no power at all.
3. Your power base depends on your aspiration, or expectation level.

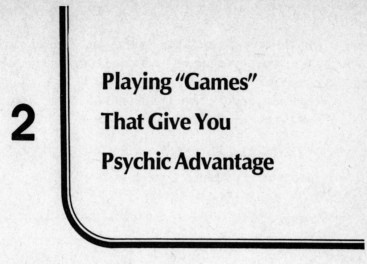

Playing "Games"
That Give You
Psychic Advantage

You are either gaining ground in your effort to attain psychic advantage over others or you are losing it.

This is so because of a law of nature that says that you either progress in your individual development or you fall back. Rarely do you stand still.

Thus, gaining a high degree of psychic advantage entails constant effort. And much of this effort can be directed at observing the "games" people play to gain control of people and situations.

Developing your own plan

They play them everywhere — in the office and the home, in marriage and courtship, in church and in politics, in fact, in virtually every phase of life.

What are these games, and how are they played? Once you become a practitioner of psychic advantage, you will come to your own conclusions and evolve your own "game plan."

41

But for now, we're going to give you a head start. In this chapter, we're going to observe some of the more popular games in action.

There are innumerable benefits to be gained from mastering these games, including:

- Greater income.
- Increased power.
- Elevated status.
- Stronger security.

Some of the more popular tactics I've used and seen in action include:

- Developing your own style.
- Winning at office-manship.
- Advancing through communication style.
- Maintaining a high visibility.

Let's discuss each of these.

Developing your own style

What is your natural "style?" Is it helping or hurting your chances of gaining control over people and situations? These are questions you'll have to come to grips with before you can attain a high degree of psychic advantage.

Certainly there's no pat formula, no universally acceptable style that will guarantee you success. In most cases, it's a matter of trial and error, of evolving a style that you *can* comfortably live with. To be effective, that style must be used in connection with your distinct personality and temperament.

How Joe Gordon gets results

Joe Gordon uses an authoritarian approach in his dealings with people.

"Actually, Joe seems a little brash to some people," a long-time associate said. "But that's because he's open and up-front. When you get to know him, you realize that his candor is really honesty."

This honesty is precisely what gives Joe control over many people and situations. Being indirect and sometimes devious themselves, other people automatically respond to such refreshing openness.

At work, both peers and subordinates usually go out of their way to get the job done for Joe. Here, too, he enjoys a high degree of control.

Why Joe's approach works

Why does this authoritarian approach work so well for Joe? "Basically for two reasons," he said. "First, it's a natural style for me. I'm up front with people, and I expect them to be that way with me.

"Second, there's this matter of what makes people tick. I happen to think that *fear* is a prime motivator, as long as you're otherwise fair and consistent in your leadership style."

Brownlee believes in showmanship

Walt Brownlee, national sales director for a major distillery, is another authoritarian type who subscribes to pretty much the same philosophy. He believes, however, that there's showmanship in salesmanship and often uses this idea to get his point across rather dramatically.

For example, when Walt's salespeople don't reach their quotas, they know things are going to happen at the next sales meeting. In one meeting, for example, Walt walked in late (giving his salespeople time to increase their apprehension). Then he entered with a flair, kicking a wastepaper basket across the floor and throwing a small stool against the wall to get their attention.

Candidate for an Oscar?

"Walt then ranted and raved like a madman," one of his veteran producers said. "He paced the floor constantly, all the while gesticulating like a Shakespearean actor. It was really a first-class acting job. I know it was acting, because many times after one of his 'performances,' he'd walk into his boss's office and say, 'That was quite a show I put on today, wasn't it? Think I ought to be a nominee for an Oscar?'"

So how did this bit of thespian gamesmanship give Walt greater control?

"Well, it terrorized the younger salesmen," a veteran salesman said, "and almost without exception, their sales went up the next month. And even the old-timers, who were of course familiar with the act, perked up a bit in their sales volume. You'd have to say the overall effect was positive."

So if you're a pretty good actor and capable of throwing a believable temper tantrum here and there, this can be a most effective power game — one that is almost certain to enhance your power position among your fellows.

How Bellows uses "soft" style

Obviously, not everyone can play this type of game. For example, Harry Bellows is a mild-mannered, rather soft-spoken accountant who uses just the opposite approach. He feels the "soft" approach is more in keeping with his personality and thus more effective *for him.*

Harry speaks so softly that if he's any distance away, one must literally lean forward to hear what he is saying. It is a technique he learned during his brief career as a salesman some years ago. He would talk very softly on a critical point, forcing the prospect to lean forward to hear what he was saying. He would then put the contract in front of the prospect and hand him a pen with which to sign it.

Why people strain to listen

At work, Harry is trying to get his people to "sign" another form of "contract," one that obligates them to give a top performance.

The technique is effective because of Harry's velvet touch. But in reality, he is as tough, if not tougher, than Joe Gordon when it comes to dealing with problem people.

There is a more subtle, but potentially as effective, off-shoot of the authoritarian "game." This one is a bit of dirty pool, so to speak. But as you've no doubt already surmised, psychic advantage games aren't always fair. Someone "loses," and it's usually the person who neither understands the nature of psychic advantage nor knows how to use it. Here's how it works.

How Jones "handles" Smith

Jones is director of operations for a computer company. He is insecure in his position for a number of reasons and feels he's going to be asked to take early retirement. One of the main reasons for his apprehension is Smith, a younger employee in the department who, it appears, is being groomed as a possible replacement for Jones.

Being privy to company proprietary information, Jones finds out that one of the company's out-of-town subsidiaries is about to get in trouble because of quality-control problems.

Realizing the magnitude of the problem, Jones sees a chance to improve his position and, at the same time, reduce Smith's. The conversation goes like this:

How Jones gains advantage

Jones: Smith, I'd like for you to take a few days off and spot-check our operation in Midland.

Smith: Any particular reason?

Jones: Apparently nothing serious. Just having a little trouble with quality. Ought to be right down your line.

Smith: Fine. I'll leave Monday. How long will it take?

Jones: Well, I want you back Thursday for the safety meeting. That'll give you three whole days.

Smith: Sounds reasonable.

Jones: Great. I'll inform the president that we hope to have the quality situation cleared up in Midland by Thursday.

Smith: You can depend on it.

Smith sees the light

Only after he starts delving into the quality problem at Midland does Smith realize he's on what is more like a three-month rather than a three-day assignment. Meanwhile, Jones has notified the president that Smith should have the situation cleared up in three days.

When Smith returns and reports that the project will take much longer, Jones appears not to have known the magnitude of the job.

But it matters not. The damage has been done. Jones leaves the president with the impression that Smith blew it. He tells Smith, "Well, sorry you couldn't handle it. I guess it was just too big a job for you."

As a result of this little gamesmanship, Jones gains power and Smith loses it. But Smith, now the wiser for the effort, has added a little psychic advantage game to his own repertoire — one that he will no doubt practice one day on some unsuspecting young man on his way up.

Harvey Simpson's case

Harvey Simpson, sales manager for a service organization, used a similar technique to extract the "last ounce of effort" from his salesmen.

Harvey hired a bright young salesman and assigned him to what was supposed to be one of the company's "best" territories.

At least this is the distinct impression Harvey gave. Actually, the territory was one of the most geographically far-flung and, in that respect, the least productive in the company.

Thus it was that Harvey's goal, or quota, $500,000 in sales and 10 percent in new accounts, was made to seem realistic.

The salesman "fails"

Naturally, the salesman fell short of his goal, reaching only $475,000 in sales and roughly 8 percent in new customers. It was, in fact, a superior first-year effort, one that *should* have given Harvey considerable leverage in his salary negotiation.

But Harvey, the crafty sales manager, maintained psychic advantage throughout. "You're getting close," he advised his new salesman. "Another year and you ought to be reaching your goals. *Then* we can talk about that raise."

Winning at office-manship

As Vance Packard pointed out some time ago, you can look at a person's possessions and tell roughly where he or she stands in the business world.

Real game players like Ted Lane recognize the value of status symbols and use them whenever they can to enhance their psychic advantage base. The status game is played with fervor in most offices and aptly deserves the label of *office-manship*. Here's a recent incident that illustrates the point.

Ted is a media specialist in an advertising and public relations firm. There are about 20 people in the company, all about equal in rank except for the owner and his first lieutenant.

How offices reflect status

These two occupy corner offices, with views in two directions. Their offices are large, and they are furnished with mahogany desks, comfortable sofas, and plush chairs.

Ted occupies the office next to the owner's, not by chance but by very definite *design*. It seems that in the normal course of business Ted found many "reasons" for making trips to the owner's office. One was to get the owner's approval of the company newsletter, which Ted had volunteered to write. Still another was to pass on the latest pro football odds. Another was to pick up memos and reports. And there was a host of other flimsy reasons. Ted was performing countless such tasks, none of which was listed in his "job description."

Ted moves "next door"

Ted got the office next door and thereby became — at least *geographically* — the heir apparent to the owner's job, though such assumption was not justified by Ted's tenure, ability, nor real ranking in the company.

But Ted, a first-class game player, fully realized that it is on such *assumptions* that careers are often made. It's like using part of your neighbor's yard as a shortcut for a period of years. After a certain time, the part of *his* yard that *you* have been using routinely becomes legally yours.

Game players like Ted know not only *what* office to select, but how to furnish it, when possible, with meaningful status symbols. These symbols notify the world that you're "in."

How to seek out symbols

Ted couldn't swing the more expensive furniture, but he did manage to arrange for a gold-plated pen and pencil set (the same kind used by the owner) and one small picture. These limited symbols, coupled with his office location, labeled Ted as a definite "comer."

To gain psychic advantage through office-manship, take a hard look at who has what and then act accordingly.

Ted, incidentally, was eventually elevated to the *real* number two spot in the organization. No one seemed to know precisely why. But game players fully understood the situation.

Gaining advantage through meetings

In most business, civic, and social activities, meetings are a near ritual. They're called at a moment's notice, on the slightest pretext. And just because they're such a universal means of exchanging ideas, meetings are a prime means of gaining psychic advantage.

For example, regular staff meetings are par for the course in most organizations. Let's take a look at how Bobby

Wilson, a personnel generalist, uses these sessions to further his own cause.

Bobby usually manages to arrive at the meeting first. This gives him a chance to get what he considers to be the most desirable seat — right next to the head man, who normally sits at the head of the table.

Seating yourself next to the "throne"

If you'll notice, the seat to the right or left of the head man in most meetings is usually occupied by the "number two man." "It's definitely what you might call a power position," Bobby notes. "If you make it a point to occupy that seat at staff meetings long enough, even the more powerful members in your group will begin to concede that it's *yours*. Once they begin to make this and other similar little mental concessions, you're actually a lot closer to the number two spot than you might think." Which is precisely the point of office-manship, to convince others that you are a candidate for a leading role.

Implying you're in the know

But even when he's late and someone else is occupying his number two seat, Bobby continues to play the game of musical chairs with verve and imagination.

In such cases, he somehow manages to position himself in back of or alongside the head man. This way, he can cast knowing glances at the audience, implying that he knows what the meeting's all about and he's just there as a formality. Or he can smile knowingly as the head man is about to make a key point, suggesting again that he is privy to what's going on in the upper echelons of the organization.

Late arrivals can win, too

Now, where Bobby claims to gain psychic advantage by showing up early for meetings, others apparently get some advantage by doing just the opposite, showing up late. The late-comer rushes into the meeting five to ten minutes late (usually right on schedule) and explains rather breathlessly that he's late because he was tied up in a hot deal.

This gives the impression of extreme busy-ness. In addition, the late-comer can pick his own spot at the back of the room to *stand*, implying that right after this meeting he's got to be off and running to put out another brush fire.

There are various other ways to gain psychic advantage through some other forms of office-manship.

Suggesting "intimacy" with the boss

Buddy Folsom, an up-and-coming game player, likes to give the impression that he's definitely "in the blueprint," that it's only a matter of time before he's running things.

He'll subtly manage to work in remarks to the leader — in front of the meeting, of course — such as "That's not the way we heard it on the 19th hole, is it Charley?" or "I believe we've got that one under control now, haven't we Sam?" Being an astute power player who knows just how far he can go in the power game, Buddy knows just how much of this kind of talk his leader is willing to take.

Making a splash at bigger meetings

At bigger meetings, power players often use a different tack.

Seating arrangement isn't all that important at general

meetings, though there is one popular theory that contends that you gain psychic advantage by walking faster and sitting in the front row.

This might well be. On the other hand, some power players feel they get an even greater advantage by *standing* near the *back* of the room and firing questions from that vantage point in a booming voice.

Standing gives high visibility

"It definitely gets everyone's attention," said one veteran game player. "The louder you boom your question, the faster virtually everyone in the room turns around to see who's talking. This definitely puts you in the spotlight."

Standing in certain meetings is a game played by a good many. The rationale is that if you are physically "above" another person, you have a degree of psychic advantage over him.

Just as our power-conscious friend used this tactic at general meetings, where virtually everyone else was seated, Sol Levin, a successful Texas attorney, uses it in his office transactions.

Sol Levin, "dime among nickels"

To begin with, Sol is only slightly over five feet two inches, a fact that he professes to be quite proud of. He assumes the same kind of attitude as Billy Rose, the erstwhile diminutive New York showman who barely stood over five feet. When asked how he felt among those tall leading men and stately show girls, he replied, "Like a dime among nickels."

Nonetheless, Sol tried to "rise" to the occasion whenever possible. For example, in his sumptuous office, Sol made it a point to have his visitors sit. He did so because he had had his executive swivel chair raised a full six inches, while the other chairs in the room had been cut off by at least an inch or two. In addition, the sofa and chairs were so plush that when visitors sat in them, they sank two or three more inches.

Little wonder, then, that Sol invariably insisted on "sitting down and talking things over" when it came to discussing a business deal. It was one way for him to gain psychic advantage.

Incidentally, this idea of raising seats to enhance self-esteem isn't new. It's done on occasion in the highest diplomatic circles. For instance, at the Korean peace talks, the North Koreans had their chairs built up so that they actually towered over the taller American negotiators by several inches during discussions.

Advancing through communication style

If you can gain a reputation for being a good source of information, you're on your way to attaining a high degree of psychic advantage.

At the bridge club, notice how others cling to the words of the resident gossip, the person who invariably seems to know who's having marital trouble and who's about to buy a new home or have a baby.

Randy Johnson: source of information

It works the same way for the office. For example, at a Fort Worth investment company, people usually turn to Randy Johnson, a young account executive, when they want to find out the latest scuttlebutt about the company or the people in it.

Randy didn't just stumble into this job as "town crier." He's a strong game player who has carefully cultivated his information sources over a period of years.

"No doubt about it," Randy says. "It's just like being a

good reporter. You've got to work quite hard at building up your sources."

The secretary is a solid source

"More often than not, a top executive's confidential secretary is much more than just a secretary," Randy says. "She is a confidante, administrative assistant, and probably most important of all, a sort of 'body guard.'

"Take our president's secretary, for example. She sets up all of his appointments, services all of his telephone calls, and arranges for all of his trips, among other things. All of this gives her the power to determine, to a large extent, who gets in to see the boss."

How he gets "information"

Randy, like many an enterprising young executive seeking psychic advantage, has managed to charm his way on to the secretary's "good side." He has done so with flattery, special attention, and even small gifts.

As a result, Randy's reports, telephone calls and requests for an audience with the president are handled expeditiously.

"But the real payoff in cultivating the boss's secretary comes in being privy to company 'confidential information,'" Randy says. "For example, I recently found out through our president's gal Friday that the company was thinking about opening up a new financial research section and they would be looking for someone to run it. It looked like a real opportunity, so I immediately started researching other financial companies across the country to find out what they had working in this respect. Within six months, I was somewhat of an expert in the area."

Sure enough, within the year, the company did start a

new research section. And who was named to head it? Randy, of course, who was thoroughly prepared for the job.

Undoubtedly, it pays to cultivate your sources.

On cultivating executive's secretaries

Secretaries. "These women usually have the real inside poop. Frankly, I find that a great deal of flattery and an occasional cup of coffee works best in developing these ladies as a source."

Public library. "This is a gold mine of information if you use it properly.

"Many of the metropolitan libraries have what they call a service center. These centers will answer most pertinent questions about almost anything except medical or legal issues — and in a hurry! One day my boss asked me about the performance of a certain stock over a several-year period. He was astounded when I came back with the answer within ten minutes. That's how long it took the center to come up with the information — *over the telephone.*

"What's more, most of the big libraries have major papers like *The New York Times* on microfilm. As you know, the *Times* is known as the paper of record. You can find almost anything in it."

Try public relations or personnel

Personnel department. "A valid source here is a *must.* They know, usually well in advance, about such things as promotions, transfers, policy changes, and the like."

Public relations. "Generally, these people are a good source. But though they like to snoop themselves, they're normally adverse to someone surveying *their* bailiwick. To offset this, I have learned to read upside down with some proficiency.

Thus, I go into the PR office daily on the pretext of reading *The Wall Street Journal*; then I get what I can from reading the printed material spread over their desks, and this is usually considerable. They're lousy housekeepers."

Cultivating people in key areas

Key departments. "Getting to know key employees in key departments, such as accounting, computer service, sales, and the like, is imperative — for obvious reasons."

Rest rooms. "People let it all hang out, so to speak, in the company john. If you're willing to spend a little more time than usual in a not-too-uncomfortable stall, you can pick up all sorts of interesting facts."

Become a reliable information source; then use this information to go one-up in your dealings with others. It's a shortcut to psychic advantage.

Answering a question with a question

Gathering information is clearly linked with the art of asking questions, a topic that is covered comprehensively in a later chapter.

However, one of the techniques not covered there — and one of the more effective ones used in communications — is to answer a question with a question.

Properly used, this technique is an effective way to *control* almost any interview.

The salesman as an underdog

Typically, for example, a salesman is the clear-cut underdog in his relations with clients. The client can arbitrarily "eliminate" the salesman, and he can usually find a product just as cheaply from someone else. The client normally has to be sold not only on the salesman himself, but on the product as well. Thus, he maintains a high psychic advantage going into the sales negotiation.

This makes it necessary for the salesperson to learn every trick he can to gain and keep control of the interview. One of these ways is to answer the client's question with a question, in a timely and appropriate manner.

Making questions appropriate

By appropriate we mean this: If a client were to ask, "How many units will your machine turn out an hour?" you might appropriately counter with, "Mr. Prospect, what kind of production would you like from a machine of this make?" But it would be *in*appropriate for you to respond to the same question with, "Well, Mr. Buyer, when did you expect delivery?"

The second question is irrelevant. It does not follow logically. It is intimidating to the client. Instead of helping the salesperson get client support, it alienates him. So remember, make the question appropriate.

Salesman vs. client

Let's listen in briefly to a discussion between a salesman and a client. See who, in your opinion, is controlling the interview.

Salesman: We feel we have the best office-size computer in the market. I'm sure it'll more than suit your needs.

Prospect: Could be. But frankly, we were looking for something a little more economical.

Salesman: Look, you pay for what you get. You know that, Mr. Prospect. We've got the "Cadillac of the computer business."

Prospect: Well, I don't *drive* a Cadillac. Why should I want a "Cadillac computer?"

Salesman: I just feel that once you use our computer, Mr. Prospect, you won't really be satisfied with any other. It's that superior.

Prospect: Do you think your company would give us a price break if we bought a unit for each of our five branch offices?

Salesman: Well, we don't normally offer a discount on this line. But I could check into it for you.

How a question gets commitment.

There were several places in the interview where the salesman could have turned the interview in his favor by answering the client's question with one of his own. By responding with a question, the salesman can often get a commitment from the other party. For example, let's tune in again on another interview.

Turning the interview around

Salesman: We feel that we have the best office-size computer in the market. I'm sure it'll suit all your needs.

Prospect: Could be. But frankly, we were looking for something a little more economical. How much do your machines cost?

Salesman: They vary in price, Mr. Prospect. Do you mind my asking what price range you had in mind?

Prospect: Well, frankly, we didn't want to go over $25,000, and even that's a little high.

Salesman: Well, our 321-P model falls in the $18,000 to $23,000 price range, depending on attachments. It's not quite as sophisticated as the model I just demonstrated, but it's just as efficient. I think it'll suit your needs just as well as the other for the time being.

Prospect: That would be more in line with what we had in mind. You know, I was thinking...we have five branch offices...could we get a discount price by buying five units?

Salesman: That's possible, Mr. Prospect. Would you like me to inquire about a special discount price on five units?

Prospect: Why yes, I wouldn't mind just *seeing* what kind of price I could get.

Salesman: Fine. I'll check on that today and be back to you tomorrow. Would afternoon or evening be best for me to get back to you?

Prospect: Afternoon, I suppose. Make it 3 o'clock.

Why the technique works

Why is the answer-a-question-with-a-question technique effective here? Because it gets a *commitment* from the other person. The client has said that he's interested in the $18,000 to $23,000 model and that he's further interested in the discount price. You know these things because you *asked*. The sale is almost made.

Maintaining high visibility

George Jones is a public relations representative for a big Dallas distributor. As such, he has relatively high visibility in the company. He is generally regarded to be smart, capable, and a fast worker.

Despite such virtues, George didn't receive a single promotion during his first five years with the company. Why? Well, the reason isn't something that is likely to appear on an employee appraisal form.

Solving George's appearance problem

George, you see, was grossly overweight; he had the general appearance of a stuffed walrus. And he was a sloppy dresser to boot. In short, you might say that George had an image problem.

His clothes were expensive enough, but somehow they almost always had the appearance of having been slept in. His ties — when he wore them — didn't match his suits. And then there were those ankle-length socks! Every time he crossed his legs, he revealed a huge hunk of flesh between the tops of the socks and his trousers. Gross!

Now, if you're saying, "Well, what has all this got to do with the man's *talent?*" forget it. As one of the leading executive recruiters in the Southwest said, "Grooming and general appearance, including the way a person is dressed, account for as much as 80 percent of his or her success in landing a good job." And, he should have added, for holding one.

Best friends: Hart, Schaffner & Marx

Fortunately for George, he "straightened up" when he married a woman who was clothes conscious. This lends credence to a couple of myths: one, that opposites do sometimes marry; and two, that women often marry men to convert them in one way or another — sartorially in this instance.

"No doubt about it," George said. "Three of my best friends these days are *Hart, Schaffner & Marx!*" He was referring, of course, to the old and respected clothier that turns out rather expensive, high-quality suits.

George's dress philosophy these days is that it's better to have a few quality suits than lots of cheap ones. "They not only look better," he said, "but they last longer. They definitely help create a strong image."

Building an "in" wardrobe

Thanks to close guidance from his wife, George has acquired an almost entirely new wardrobe of suits in shades of blue, gray, and beige. There might be an occasional black or brown one around, but for the most part he selects conservative "in" colors that most successful business and professional people wear.

His ties now match his suits. For the most part, they include smart diagonal stripes and conservative patterns, worn mainly with striped suits, and a few floral design ties for plain suits.

One of George's dress problems was his penchant for colored and patterned shirts, worn with bright patterned ties. He eliminated this problem, by and large, by switching to white shirts, mostly button-down. White shirts have made a strong "comeback" in many prestige companies.

"They didn't have to 'come back' with us," said Tom Croft, senior vice president of Dallas' prestigious Republic National Bank. "We're an aggressive banking organization, but we have remained quite conservative in our dress code. We feel that white shirts reflect a stable, conservative atmosphere. Our top people wear them almost exclusively on the job."

A health regime helps, too

Clothes alone can't give you the look and feel of success. Most power people who have psychic advantage in their daily relations seem to exude a sort of vibrance that comes from a combination of good health and attitude. Many acquire this image by spending a few bucks — and a lot of effort — at a local health spa.

Most executives past 40 desperately need some sort of health regime. Some form of aerobics — regular walking, jogging, cycling, or swimming — can restore muscle tone and put bounce back in your walk. A little sunshine can add immeasurably to that vibrant look, too.

The payoff: George is a "wheel"

Incidentally, George Jones is a "wheel" these days. And he now *looks* and *feels* sharp most of the time.

"I just didn't realize," he said, "what a big difference appearance could make. I feel great these days, and at the risk of sounding immodest, I'd say I look it too."

Look good, feel good, and watch your psychic advantage increase.

KEY IDEAS

As a rule, you are either improving your psychic advantage position or you are losing ground. Rarely do you stand still.

One way to constantly move forward in your quest for more psychic advantage is to learn to play the power "games" that people play — using your own inimitable style, of course. You can do so by:

- *Developing your own style.*
  - Manage equally well with either an authoritarian approach or a "velvet-touch" approach.
- *Learning to win at office-manship.*

- Use status symbols discreetly.
- Discover how to use office arrangement and location.
- Master the art of becoming highly visible at meetings.
- Perfect the technique of "elevation."

- *Improving your "communication style."*
  - Cultivate executive secretaries and other key sources of information.
  - Go one-up by answering a question with a question.

- *Learning to dress your way to success.*
  - Look sharp, feel sharp, be sharp.

3

How to Develop Psychic Advantage by Finding and Pushing Hot Buttons

To gain psychic advantage over others, you need to find out what makes them tick. You can do this by discovering their basic needs and then playing up — or down — to these needs as the situation dictates.

Salespeople sometimes call these needs "hot buttons." "People tend to buy emotionally," one veteran salesman said. "Comfort, prestige, convenience — these are the hot buttons that cause most people to finally buy. If you can find a client's hot button, you can usually make the sale."

Button-finding isn't easy

But, he hastened to add, finding a hot button is normally not an easy thing to do. On the contrary, it's usually quite difficult. It entails your really listening to what the other person says (and doesn't say), genuinely observing his actions, and accurately perceiving his attitudes. All this is a big order, even for a highly skilled communicator.

A hot button can be translated into specific benefits such as health, prestige, and comfort, among others. But for practical purposes, we're grouping all such benefits under four broad categories:

- Need for well-being.
- Need for self-esteem.
- Need to achieve.
- Need to know and understand.

Once you're able to recognize and exploit these needs in others, you'll be able to find ingenious ways to use them to gain psychic advantage over others.

Using the need for well-being

We're talking here about such basic physical needs as food, water, and sex, plus the deep-seated need for safety and security. All of these factors add up to a sense of well-being, and each can be used as a prime hot button to gain control over others.

Sex can be one of the hottest buttons of all. Nations use it to gain power over other nations. Corporations use it to gain an edge in competition. Businessmen use it to gain control over clients. And husbands and wives have forever used it to gain psychic advantage in the perennial battle of the sexes.

Exploiting physiological needs

In an affluent society, one in which business is trying to accommodate *higher* human needs, you would think that the more basic needs would offer little motivation.

But the basic physiological needs, if unmet, can create problems, as is shown in this incident, which took place at an Oklahoma electronics firm.

The company is located in an abandoned World War II air base, about 20 miles from any populated area.

Because of its remoteness, the company pays premium wages, a good 15 percent above most other industrial companies in the area. The firm offers excellent fringe benefits, and working conditions are good.

Despite this happy combination of factors, the general manager of the division noticed what he considered generally poor morale.

An attitude survey gets at the problem

"There were the usual indicators of poor morale, including high absenteeism, above-average scrap and rework, and general griping," the manager said. "But more than that, it was the strong undercurrent of dissatisfaction that you could *feel* when trying to relate to the work force."

Perplexed as to the reason for the discontent, the company resorted to an expensive attitude survey.

The survey revealed the problem — the eating facilities. Since there were no restaurants nearby, most of the employees ate from the food-service truck that came by daily. The quality of the food was reflected in the nickname employees pinned on the truck — "roach coach."

Problem is solved

The problem was corrected, and morale seemed to improve virtually overnight. "We overlooked a basic need, and it put us at a real disadvantage," the manager concluded.

The need for safety and security

Strong as the sexual drive is, it can sometimes take a back seat to the compelling need for safety and security. Some years ago, the wife of a wealthy industrialist had a fling with a dashing, but poor, young playwright. Learning of the affair, the industrialist gave her a choice between "love" and security with him. She opted for the latter. Having detected her *dominant* hot button, the industrialist used this knowledge to control his errant spouse throughout the remainder of the marriage.

This need for safety and security is a bona fide hot button that affects most of us in our workaday world on an almost continuous basis. The chances of using this hot button to gain control of people and situations are interesting and seemingly infinite.

Charley Young's story

The case of a salesman illustrates the point. The salesman is Charley Young. He's a commissioned salesman now, making more money than he's ever made before. But it wasn't always that way.

During the first few years of his sales career, Charley worked on a salary plus, in some cases, a small commission. His salary during that time was "average" for the field he was in.

"This is what bugged me," Charley said. "I kept hearing about these fabulous incomes in the sales field, and here I was with an average income."

Pie-in-the-sky ads

"Sure, I know the newspapers were full of sales jobs where the 'sky was the limit.' But that's the problem. I always felt they were 'pie-in-the-sky' ads, and that's why I didn't try them."

True, many such ads are strictly blue sky. But what Charley was not willing to admit to himself was the *real* reason for his not launching into *any* of these strictly commission jobs, and that was a strong sense of *in*security.

Charley had grown up in the Depression, and the need for a "fixed income" prevented him from trying the more lucrative sales jobs.

Al Sankary "converts" Charley

Who turned Charley's thinking around? Al Sankary, a friend and long-time commissioned manufacturer's representative.

"I tried to talk Charley into coming with me for several years," Al said. "I was successful in doing so only after I convinced him of his obsession with this security business. I convinced him the only security is in yourself. Now he's a big money-maker, and I might add, a well adjusted individual."

Most big companies today add to their employees' sense of security by offering a full line of fringe benefits.

"No doubt about this," said a senior recruiter for a major oil company. "One of the standard questions today's college grad comes up with is, 'What kind of benefits package do you offer?' If you're not in line with your competitors, forget it."

The success of the union movement in this country reflects the strength of the security need. Before wide-spread unionism, many workers were exploited — long hours, poor pay, bad working conditions, and little, if any, security. The company obviously held a high degree of psychic advantage.

Unions corrected much of that, and today the typical American worker has more security than any other. Does this mean that unionism is the only way to satisfy this hot button? It definitely does not, and Malcolm Stewart shows how you can get what *you* want by helping others to get what *they* want.

How Malcolm Stewart succeeded

Stewart started his own manufacturing plant with low capitalization. He was a rugged individualist who had come up through the ranks and thoroughly understood the typical work-man and his frustrations. Employees, in turn, related well to him. As a result, the company grew rapidly, and there was relative harmony in the ranks.

However, since the company was still quite young, Stewart could not offer some of the higher wages and fringe benefits offered by some of his competitors. Unfortunately, union organizers played up this fact and were able to rally suf-ficient support to win — or so it appeared.

Stewart was obviously losing control of the situation. If his company unionized, he would obviously lose a degree of control over his people. So how did he gain control? By push-ing the same hot button the union did, only in spades.

Working through some of his older, trusted lieutenants, Stewart said: "Look, I can't offer you all of the fancy bene-fits right now. But I will be able to — and soon. In fact, ef-fective immediately, I'm starting a company-wide profit-sharing plan. As the company makes money, you make money. If we do as well as I think we're going to do, every employee who sticks with me will be able to retire with a comfortable nest egg."

Stewart's appeal worked. His personal integrity and magnetism had something to do with it. But in the end, he gained control because of his willingness to offer employees even more security than the union did. You might say, Stewart went one-up on the union in hot-buttonsmanship.

It's easy to see how an employer can keep an employee in line by *threatening* his sense of security. He can do this in any number of ways — by turning in an unsatisfactory evalua-tion, by severely criticising his work, or if the individual has a weak self-image, by simply avoiding him to a large extent in both a business and social sense. But the employer obviously has the upper hand anyway. The question is, can an *employee* gain a degree of parity by pushing the boss's security hot button? It's not easy, but it can be done. Al Simons shows us how.

Al Simons' case

Al is a junior executive in a big manufacturing company. He recognizes that *everybody* answers to somebody in a big organization. And everyone is concerned with his or her personal security. In fact, the higher you go up the hierarchy, the more concerned you must be.

Naturally, Al says, you'll want to do everything you can to help your immediate boss satisfy his security needs. "He rightfully expects this and can make it rough if he discovers you are working against his needs," Al said. But it is precisely such a circumstance that can give you a chance to gain psychic advantage.

"To gain this advantage," Al said, "you must find out exactly what it takes to make your boss's boss secure. For example, my boss had a little over two years of college. Not that that has anything to do with his ability. He's super competent. But *his* boss has a Master's Degree in Business Administration and even did a little college work beyond that. The point is, he's sort of a nut on education.

Gaining control by degrees

"When I found this out, I immediately started working on my Master's Degree at night school. Now, on the surface, this might seem a bit intimidating to my immediate boss, and perhaps it was to a degree. But what I had come to realize was that when the big boss asked my boss whom he was grooming as a replacement for his job, he would likely have to throw my name in the hopper because of my advanced degree. All things being equal, the Master's Degree would give me a better shot at the job. So I would say that this action gave me a subtle — and of course limited — 'control' over my immediate boss."

Al continued: "I've found that another way to gain psychic advantage over a superior is to take over more and more of his work. You can say, 'Look boss, you shouldn't be handling this kind of menial stuff. Let me take care of it for you.'"

Delegating the way to control

Bosses are usually more than willing to delegate every detail they can. The point is, if you can get him to delegate enough of these small chores, you will soon have most of the "answers" about his job. When the big boss calls down for information or an opinion, your boss will immediately turn to you for the answers, simply because he's delegated his way out of knowing offhand what the answers are.

While it's probably true that no man is indispensable in any organization, this does not preclude your being next to indispensable to your immediate boss. Once he routinely starts to turn to you for answers and opinions on subjects vital to your function, you've gained yourself a degree of psychic advantage. If you play your cards right, it can lead to something big for you.

The need for self-esteem

Ego might well be the biggest little word in the dictionary.

We all have one, and we almost always like to have it massaged. Indeed, the need for self-esteem is so great that virtually every self-improvement book of significance is built around the general theme of developing a worthy self-image.

Each of us has an image of ourself, formed over the years by the sum total of our life experiences. Normally that image is characterized as "high" or "low," or perhaps in between. However, that image is rarely constant. It goes up and down in the course of daily activities. If the boss pats us on the back, our self-image soars; if he chews us out, it drops perceptibly. The degree of fluctuation depends on the strength of the image.

To gain psychic advantage over another, it is necessary to find out how to manipulate his or her self-image, to make the other's self-image go up or down as the situation warrants. The three factors that you can use over and over to do this are *status, prestige,* and *opportunity for achievement.*

Satisfying status needs

How do you go about gaining psychic advantage by using status? Do you build up a person's ego by extolling his virtues? Or do you whittle him down to size by delivering deadly blows to his ego? Actually, either way will work. It depends entirely on the individual and circumstances involved.

For example, put yourself momentarily into the shoes of Cliff Johnson, manager of a medium-sized service organization. Cliff has a "personnel problem" in Sid Pemberton, a middle-aged class B clerk who has been with the company for 17 years. Since Sid obviously is not considered management material, he has been passed over for promotion countless times. Each time he is passed over, his morale — and production — seems to drop a bit lower. Not low enough to get him fired, mind you, for he takes care to barely fulfill his job requirements. Besides, Sid has high seniority. If you were Cliff, how would you resolve the problem?

Power is limited

Cliff is boss and thus holds the psychic advantage, since he has the power to fire Sid. But his power and control are limited somewhat for a couple of reasons. It would take an extremely well-documented case to fire Sid. And besides, Sid *is* a knowledgeable worker whose experience is badly needed in a department that has a high turnover problem. So in a sense, you might say Cliff's control is limited in that he would have a hard time firing Sid. And even if he could, he would be reluctant to do so because of Sid's departmental experience.

Cliff finally decided that the best way to salvage Sid as a productive employee was to appeal strongly to his status need — to repair his badly eroded self-esteem. No doubt about it, the job had become a "downer" for Sid.

Cliff called Sid into his office for a chat. "Sid," he said, "you've been with us for 17 years now, and you've been a steady and loyal employee. I've talked it over with the boss, and he feels as I do. We ought to use your experience more fully around the department. Since you know more about the history of the group than just about anyone, we thought we'd appoint you as our *clerical consultant.* You can answer some of the questions and help us solve lots of the problems that come up around here every day. There'll be a modest raise to go with it. How do you think you would feel about such an arrangement?"

Of all the words that Cliff spoke, only two stood out boldly in Sid's mind — *clerical consultant.* The "modest raise" barely registered, but words like "use your experience more fully" and "steady and loyal employee" made a tremendous impression on Sid.

In this case, I think you can safely conclude that Cliff gained greater control of the person — and the situation — by pushing Sid's status hot button. After all, Cliff's job is to get things done through people, and he now has one more person working for him "full time."

Fortunately, business and industry have caught on. They now know that money isn't the only motivator. In fact, the farther one goes up the managerial ladder, the more one regards money as a token of worth rather than an indicator of intrinsic economic value. At a certain level, prestige, status, and room for growth become far more important as motivators to most executives.

Titles don't cost much

The beauty of it is, you don't normally have to be high on the organizational totem pole to get a title. For example, most thinking organizations rarely have custodians any more, they have sanitary engineers. In industry, people on the assembly line aren't inspectors, they're quality-control engineers. Many others, like Sid, are not simply clerks or workers, but consultants. Salesmen aren't peddlers any more, they're representatives, while repairmen and technicians have become communications specialists. All of this recognition usually costs companies very little, if anything, but nets them a great deal in loyalty and performance.

Using status symbols

Bestowing a title isn't the only way to push another's esteem hot button. Status symbols often hold at least equal importance, especially in the upper levels of management. Office location (corner offices are at a premium) and furnishings (mahogany desks, pictures, television sets, and so on) can be every bit as important as money itself.

Where Cliff Johnson appealed to Sid Pemberton's esteem hot button in a positive way, he found it necessary to handle a professional employee like Roger Hamilton, an engineer, quite differently. You might say he used a "negative" manner.

An "opposite" case

Like Sid Pemberton, Roger was turning in a generally lackluster performance. But unlike Pemberton, it was not because of a lack of talent or managerial ability. In fact, Roger graduated from college with honors and appeared to have the makings of a top management man. But for some reason, he was not performing anywhere near his potential.

Cliff's counsel with Roger took quite a different turn. "Look," he said during Roger's semi-annual employee evaluation, "you've been with us two years now, and I think we ought to take a look at where we're going. You've got the background and the mind and personality to go places. But I don't understand it. Your job performance has been strictly average. You've had far too many days off, and I get the impression from your fellow employees that you're not being overly cooperative."

"Shock treatment" motivates

Such words would not normally be calculated to instill confidence and build self-esteem, but that's precisely what they did in this case. Roger was "shocked" into a conscious awareness of his plight and resolved to use his God-given talents more productively. He was soon enrolled in the company's executive development program and found himself on his way up in the organization.

Cliff should be given credit for handling this delicate situation professionally. It was the promise of room for growth — for achievement — that converted Roger into a valuable asset. Cliff emerged with more control over his problem employee than he had ever had before.

Using prestige to motivate

Many salesmen find that prestige is one of the dominant factors that cause people to buy. For example, Nita Boswell, one of the Southwest's leading real estate salesladies, uses this hot button as the basis for most of her sales in the affluent Houston area. "I always try to find out who the neighbors will be," Nita said. "Then if I see the property is right for my prospects — and I feel that prestige is important to them — I simply mention that Dr. Jones, the neurosurgeon, lives down the street and that the next door neighbor is a prominent banker. This sort of thing. I feel this strategy gives me a great deal of control over the situation, since all things being equal, prestige causes most of them to buy a particular property."

How Summers succeeds

James Summers, advertising manager for a large interior decorating firm, is one of the prime reasons his company is enjoying a meteoric growth rate. Reason: He knows how to appeal to the human need for prestige.

Sue Brothers, one of the firm's leading salesladies, readily admits that she calls on Summers when competition for business gets toughest.

Handling the "tough" ones

"We have no problem selling smaller jobs, such as homes and apartments," Sue says. "The problem comes on the big commercial jobs, where competition really gets fierce. This is where we like to call on James Summers, and in a high percentage of cases, he helps us land the job."

How does Summers maintain such a high batting average on the big jobs — in effect, gain psychic advantage over really tough-minded customers? By appealing to the customer's desire for prestige.

Painting a pretty "picture"

"Look," Summers tells a client torn between several major competitors, "you people have a beautiful building here. It's got such great possibilities, in fact, that I think I can virtually assure you we can use it in some of our company's major tie-in campaigns."

Summers then proceeds to paint a vivid word picture of how the client's building is going to look in color in a major trade publication, or perhaps on a highway billboard.

Summers' philosophy in a nutshell: People — and companies — like to feel important. Give them a chance to enhance their prestige, and they'll respond favorably almost every time.

Competitors can help

The need to achieve is clearly tied in with man's competitive nature. If you can find a way to appeal to this human desire, there is a very strong chance you can achieve a high degree of psychic advantage.

Charles Schwab got results in the steel industry many years ago by appealing to the workers' competitive nature, by pitting one shift in a steel mill against another.

For example, he drew a huge figure on the factory floor representing the first shift's output. When second-shifters saw the number, they accepted the challenge. At the end of their shift, they replaced the first-shift's number with their higher one. The race was on.

Walter Kelly, a prominent Texas Realtor, transformed his "lethargic sales force" into a hard-hitting one in somewhat the same way.

Puts names on billboard

For a nominal rental fee, he secured advertising on a billboard located on a busy artery leading into the downtown area. At the end of each month, he would post his leading salespeoples' names, along with a brief message, such as "A new company record."

What was the net effect of this gesture? "Tremendous," Kelly said. "My sales volume — from virtually the same sales force — almost tripled within the year. I'm almost certain the salesman of the month gets almost as much satisfaction from seeing his name in 'lights' as he does from making big money."

The need for achievement

Ross Ambrose has been an industrial engineer with a Fortune 500 company for the past 15 years. He and his family live in an upper-middle income neighborhood, belong to a local country club, and generally live the good life.

Ross is supervisor in charge of the company's suggestions program. By and large, the job is pretty cut-and-dried. As supervisor, Ross delegates a great deal of his work. Mainly, he handles budgets, planning, and the tougher problems that come along. He has probably reached the height of his career, which he describes as a "comfortable rut."

Despite this seemingly satisfactory state of affairs, Ross is rather disenchanted. He is like countless thousands who are plagued with what has been described philosophically as "divine discontent."

Self-actualizing! What it is and how to use it

Behavioral psychologists say this feeling of discontent is caused by a basic human need they call "self-actualization." Simply stated, this means that you must by nature do what you are intended to do. Otherwise, these feelings of discontent surface and become increasingly strong so long as the need is unfulfilled.

Self-actualization says, in effect, that a writer must write and an actor must act; in short, a person must do what by nature he is best equipped to do, regardless of the monetary reward.

In Ross's case, the uneasiness could be easily explained. In college, Ross had at first majored in electrical engineering, a field for which he had shown a marked aptitude. But somewhere along the line, Ross switched to industrial engineering so that he could get out of school earlier. Thus, years later, the dilemma: a square peg in a round hole. Here was a technically oriented person performing mainly administrative functions. The primary reason for his discontent was that he was not given a chance to self-actualize; he was not doing what he was cut out to do by nature.

Discontent is widespread

Are there many people in business and industry who don't get a chance to self-actualize? Yes, a great many. Maybe most. And what does all of this have to do with controlling others and with gaining psychic advantage? Simply this. If you can find and push a person's achievement hot button, you can gain a large measure of control over his or her performance.

You see the principle at work in virtually all walks of life; in the typical American home for example.

George "wears the pants"

Doris gives her husband George the impression that *he* is running the show. And in a sense, he is. George makes most of the major decisions. He controls the family finances. He decides where the children will go to school. But in this case, Doris is neither dumb nor passive; she is simply giving her husband a chance to self-actualize.

This idea might be frowned on by many women in this feminist era. But Doris knows her man, and she knows that "being boss" is a basic part of his makeup. So while George "wears the pants" in the family, it is Doris who really controls the relationship in many important ways. She realizes, you see, that for concessions made there must be concessions gained. So what does she have to show for all this? Only a new sports car, membership in a tennis club, a yearly vacation to an exotic spot of her choice, and lots of tender loving care. So who *really* has psychic advantage in this relationship? My vote goes to Doris, hands down.

Dealing with your boss

The boss-subordinate relationship affords one of the better areas for pushing the achievement hot button, though the technique should be used selectively. One expert opinion is that only from 5 to 10 percent of the population has high achievement needs. Not everyone, in other words, aspires to a spot in the executive suite. But the relatively few who do seek upper-management roles do so with a fervor.

The boss normally holds a clear psychic advantage over most subordinates, since he has the right to hire and fire. However, the executive who uses this power habitually finds himself leading and motivating through fear, and this is generally felt to be the least effective way to get results from others over the long haul. It is generally far more effective — and productive — to motivate by pushing an achievement hot button.

James Turner's case

James Turner is a case in point. James is personnel director for a large electronics firm. He has two young college graduates in his group who are working in entry-level jobs in the employment and labor relations sections.

Both are high-achievers. Both have outstanding records. And both, unfortunately, are becoming disgruntled over what they consider rather routine assignments.

Although James's control of the two is complete from the company viewpoint, it is limited from a practical standpoint because the two young executives have decided tentatively to take their talents elsewhere.

How is James to gain control of the situation? One option would be to tell the young men that they're being groomed for great things in the company. But such an announcement would have been premature and possibly misleading.

Instead, James decided the wiser course of action was to attempt to push their achievement hot buttons. His appraisal of the situation was that both were among the 5 to 10 percent of the population's high-achievers.

This he did by putting both of them on job-rotation throughout the plant. They were delighted with the decision, since it opened up new challenges and new vistas for growth. Both completed the rotation schedule and went on eventually to managerial posts in the organization.

Some people want an easy job. But there are some, like these two, who are constantly looking for new challenges. It's their prime hot button, and James was perceptive enough to recognize this fact and do something about it. Needless to say, it gave him greater control in the matter.

The need to know and understand

Curiosity can kill a cat, but it can also help you gain psychic advantage over others.

People are usually curious about things they don't know or understand. Someone summed up the idea years ago by observing that *knowledge is power*. Thus, an excellent way to gain control over others is to become the *source* of valuable information. This is how George Sims, a public relations writer, worked his way into the executive hierarchy in a major corporation. He became proficient at what we'll call *sourcemanship*.

Sourcemanship in action

George gained a reputation for being "in the know." In many respects, the reputation was justified. George did deal with all levels of management in carrying out his assignments. On occasion, he even had to get news releases and articles cleared through the chairman of the board. Thus, George was able to acquire information that most others in the company did not have access to. This included up-to-the-minute facts about impending transfers and moves, production, and departmental and company policy changes — all of which came to George's attention fairly early in the game.

George was at first simply delighted to be considered a good source of information. He felt important when rank-and-file employees as well as executives sought him out for "confidential" information. And in the end, it was his ability to furnish executives with such information that gave him psychic advantage and earned him a solid promotion.

Executives covet information

George's strategy can be employed in almost any big organization, where communication can be ranked anywhere from "poor" to "nonexistant." Faulty organization is partially to blame, but the human factor is almost always prevalent. It is a basic truth that people in these organizations, especially in the managerial ranks, covet information because it gives them a sense of power and well-being. Mainly for this reason, George was able to further his own cause by being "in the know." Here's how.

Rumor had it that George's company was about to undergo a drastic reorganization. Top executives are sometimes especially vulnerable to such changes, since functions are either dropped or combined in the movement, often affecting some executives adversely.

This case was no exception. The vice president of marketing was especially concerned, since rumor had it that his operation would be combined with sales, probably eliminating his function.

George became privy to information about the move. Sensing this, the vice president of marketing began to badger him for some inside information. At first, George refused to talk about the reorganization, feeling that this would be a breach of protocol and, in any case, give the vice president an edge in the power struggle that was sure to ensue.

However, it was at this point that George began to see how having valuable information could help him further his own ends. If he could swap his information for personal gain, why not? He approached the vice president discreetly with his plan and got his word that if things went right, there *would* be "something in it for George." This exchange ultimately resulted in George's promotion.

On other occasions, doling out "confidential" information can be an effective way to get cooperation from others — and, of course, a greater degree of control.

For example, let's assume you're the director of budgets and your job is to inform all department heads that they will be asked to reduce their budgets by 10 percent.

Obviously, some department heads are unwilling to make such a change. However, they might be more inclined to accept the new situation if they know *why* the reductions are being made. In this instance, it might give you a greater degree of control — and greater cooperation — if you explain to the more recalcitrant heads that the cuts are required for a futuristic project designed to get the organization out of its economic doldrums. In such a case, you are clearly working for the other person's basic need to know and understand.

KEY IDEAS

Appealing to others' basic human needs, or *hot buttons,* is a shortcut to psychic advantage.

You can control people and situations by:

- *Filling the need for well-being*
  - Satisfy physiological needs
  - Meet safety and security needs
- *Filling the need for self-esteem*
  - Give others a chance to shine
  - Elevate others' status
- *Filling the need for achievement*
  - Permit others to realize their worth
  - Exploit the value of prestige
- *Filling the need to know and understand*
  - Use *sourcemanship* to gain advantage
  - Recognize the power of information

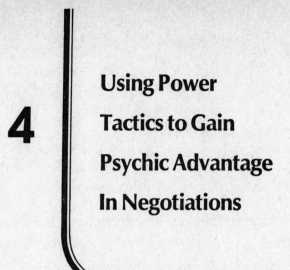

4

Using Power Tactics to Gain Psychic Advantage In Negotiations

To earn a high degree of psychic advantage in your relations with others, you need to become a master negotiator.

This doesn't mean that you'll necessarily be called on to mediate labor disputes for General Motors. It *does* mean that you need to become adept at using some of the same tactics and strategies professional mediators employ.

Negotiation, in the broad sense in which we are using the term, is involved in any relationship with another in which you try to change his or her opinion or attitude. On this basis, life is virtually a continuous negotiation with one party or another.

Learning techniques of the pros

How *well* you negotiate will depend in large measure on how successfully you can learn — and use — techniques used by professional negotiators from all walks of life.

The benefits of becoming a skillful negotiator are many. With practice you can learn to:

- Outmaneuver your competitors.
- Outwit your boss.
- Outsmart your enemies.
- Outlast your spouse (or whatever).
- Outfinesse your friends.

Specifically, in this chapter we'll discuss how to sustain a high degree of control in your negotiations by learning:

- How to use limited authority to gain psychic advantage.
- How association can put you in the driver's seat.
- How patience is the quiet way to gain control.

How to use limited authority to gain psychic advantage

Most of us respect authority. We minded our parents growing up, obeyed our teachers in school, and now conform to company rules. On the surface, then, it would seem that to have authority is to have psychic advantage. Generally, this is probably true. But not always, and herein lies a seemingly paradoxical principle: *You can gain psychic advantage in your dealings with others by having limited authority.* In other words, you can gain power by denying it.

How Frank Chambers uses authority

This principle is used frequently, and in several variations, by Frank Chambers, director of engineering for an aerospace conglomerate. In his position, Frank must routinely deal with government and military officials about technical changes and decisions on aircraft. Most of the officials have at least equal leverage.

Let's assume, for instance, that Frank is about to conclude a long and rough negotiation with a tough-minded Air
Force general who is seeking wholesale changes on a jet aircraft.

General sticks to his guns

General: Very well, Frank, we'll go along with you
on the cost changes. However, we're sticking firm on our
demand for engineering changes. I know it'll take lots of
work, but we've simply got to have them to get the kind ᴏf
plane we want.

Frank: Looks good to me. Let me run it by the
board chairman, and I should have an answer for you right
away.

General: Board chairman? You mean *you* can't
make the decision?

Frank: No. It's company policy — a new one. The
chairman has to approve any change of this magnitude.

General: This is for the birds. I thought you people
were negotiating in good faith.

Frank: I know how you feel. But look, I'll get things
squared away as soon as I can.

The general, who *can* make final decisions, seems to
have a clear advantage over Frank, who cannot. But does he?

By having limited authority to make a decision, Frank
has been able to say no gracefully. He can, if he is a good
enough actor, even hint that "I'm with you guys 100 percent.
But you know how our people at the top are. They have to stick
their noses in everything."

How Frank gains advantage

Thus, Frank gains a degree of psychic advantage by not
being able to make the final decision. He gains strength by successfully passing the buck. He can complain to the general

about his "meddlesome management," or he can protest to management about the "overbearing general."

But what, as sometimes happens, if the issue cannot be resolved and must be turned over to a third-party consultant? Doesn't Frank default his control to an outsider?

He does, in a sense, since consultants rarely understand the subtleties of the issues. Then he can complain: "After all, it's those ill-informed consultants who are screwing things up."

How a broker uses limited authority

Having limited authority appears, at first glance, to work against a real estate broker's best interests. He frequently gets caught between the seller (who wants too much) and the buyer (who offers too little). Thus, he would seem to have little psychic advantage in such negotiations.

But Stan Kubiak, a successful Oklahoma broker, has learned to use limited authority to full advantage. At the outset, he gets the seller to set a price below which he will not go under any circumstances; he also gets a top-dollar figure the seller would like to have.

Gaining psychic advantage

Stan then gets the seller to give him full negotiating rights. This means that he can, if he chooses, negotiate the entire transaction by himself. If the buyer's price is out of line, he can counter with: "The seller has instructed me not to bring an offer *that* low." Thus, limited authority actually gives Stan a degree of psychic advantage in this relationship.

Using an artificial limit to get results

There are variations of the limited authority concept. One is the *artificial limit* technique used by Jack Leverett, a buyer for a leading department store chain. In this instance, he used this approach, along with pure limited authority, to maintain the upper hand over a very aggressive salesman who was trying to sell an extra large lot of merchandise to the store.

"In that large a lot," Jack asked, "what would your price be?"

"We can give you a big break at that volume," the salesman said. "I'll just make it a flat $50,000, and it's all yours."

"Oh, oh!" Jack replied ominously. "Just as I expected, I'm out of luck. The company has budgeted me for a maximum of $45,000. Too bad. Looks like it's out of the question."

"You didn't tell me about any limit in our earlier discussions," the salesman said.

"I didn't have any idea we'd be talking about these kinds of figures," Jack replied. "At any rate, that's the top dollar, and there's not a thing I can do about it."

Bringing the price down

"I see," the confused salesman replied. "But hold on now. Let's see if there's any way we can get together. Maybe we can knock out a few frills here and there and get this thing down to your price."

Who has control of the situation at this point? Jack does, of course. By setting up a fictitious budget, Jack has successfully transferred his problem to the salesman. It is the salesman who must now figure out a way to get the price down. And in so doing, he will most likely reveal to Jack many inside facts about the transaction that Jack would not otherwise have found out about. All because Jack had limited authority to negotiate, in the first place.

Mastering the missing man technique

Jack could have — and in fact often does — use another variation of limited authority. Some negotiators call it the *missing man* approach.

Let's assume in this case that for some reason or another Jack would have been unable to use a price limit, real or artificial. The negotiation, when it got down to the nitty gritty, could have taken a turn like this:

"Well, this bid looks fine to me," Jack said. "Now if we can just find the old man and get his approval."

"Find him?" the salesman said.

"Yes, he's a busy, busy man," Jack responded, "and he's gone a lot, especially since we opened our South American subsidiary. In fact, there's a good chance he's down there right now."

"Any way to check?" the salesman asked, becoming noticeably wary by this time.

"Sure, I'll let you know tomorrow."

But several tomorrows come and go, and it soon becomes evident that the boss is, indeed, missing.

This puts Jack in a dominant position for several reasons. He has a firm offer in hand, but he can still negotiate with others. There's also an outside chance he can eventually force a hungry — and by now, very nervous — salesman to consider a lower offer.

Limited authority pays off

Having limited authority appears at first to diminish your power position. But in reality it can, as reflected in the foregoing cases, enhance your position in many respects. Both Frank and Jack were able to maintain good long-range relations with their opposite numbers— a position they might not have maintained had they had to make an unpopular decision.

But the real beauty of limited authority is that it can be either *real* or *imagined,* all depending on whether it profitably serves your purpose.

Other examples of limited authority

Here's how a few others might be able to use limited authority to gain real authority in everyday relations.

Secretary: I'm sorry, Mr. Jones. I realize you're an important client. But I can't set up an appointment for you with the directors without permission from the executive committee.

Banker: Frankly, I'd like to arrange a higher loan for you. But you know, it's a government regulation, and it's really out of our hands.

Salesman: I'll see what the company says. They won't let little old me make a decision on anything involving this much money.

Personnel Director: I'd certainly like to give you a bigger raise. Lord knows you deserve it. But the president has to approve it, and he's on an economy kick right now.

Broker: Personally, I think my client ought to go higher, but he claims this is his rock-bottom price.

Housewife: I'd love for you to join the new golf club, Dear, but it would wreck our budget.

Reporter: If I had my way, I'd kill the story. But you know how publishers are about these matters.

How association can put you in the driver's seat

I sometimes agree with Dale Carnegie about the prudent use of a cliché. A cliché can convey, in the fewest words possible, a rather sophisticated idea. One such hackneyed phrase, "birds of a feather flock together," represents the idea we're talking about here quite precisely.

What is association? In a nutshell, it's the mental linking of people or things that 1) are similar, 2) are opposite, or 3) habitually go together. For instance, Joe Namath reminds you of football, big reminds you of little, and ham goes right along with eggs.

By the same token, when you think of a particular individual, you tend to automatically think of those with whom he associates. Herein lies the potential power of this principle. Even if you yourself lack substantial power or prestige, *you can often gain a large degree of it by associating with those who do have it.*

How Fred used association successfully

The case of a man whom we shall call Fred (otherwise you might recognize him) gets the idea across.

Fred joined the accounting department of a large aerospace firm as a departmental assistant. Though he boasted several years' experience, Fred was not classified as a full accountant because he lacked a few credits necessary to get his business degree. Normally, this would have been a big obstacle in his progress up the managerial ladder.

But though Fred was a so-so accountant, he was an excellent socializer. For example, Fred discovered that the manager of the accounting department was tennis champion of the company's recreation association. Now Fred played an above-average game of tennis himself. His game was rusty, but he took care of that by practicing regularly for a couple of months. By the time he joined the recreation association, he was playing with gusto. When the smoke cleared from the annual company tournament, guess who reposed as doubles champions? None other than Fred and the manager of accounting.

Now social contacts aren't supposed to cut much ice when it comes to business. Though Fred and the manager were "buddies" in the tournament, the appropriate superior-subordinate relationship prevailed in the office. At first!

Gaining leverage

Fred, you see, was a consummate artist at the fine art of *associating*. He realized that he needed to link himself with some legitimate power source within the organization, preferably someone from another section who had leverage with his big boss, the manager of accounting. Thus having established a "target," he now needed a legitimate "cause."

This was not an easy task. Only someone like Fred, who had come to realize the full power of association, would have undertaken it. But how else would a relative newcomer to the company, especially one who lacked the proper academic credentials, ever be on par with his associates — much less have psychic advantage over them?

How Fred wooed the vice president

The "target" turned out to be the vice president of administration. Why? Because the vice president was the manager's boss. But how? This is where only the ingenious — and those really dedicated to gaining psychic advantage — need apply. Fred met both requirements.

In a highly structured organization, the gap between a vice president and a departmental assistant is enormous. It's normally difficult to even establish a line of communication. But Fred did it, and here's how.

He discovered that the vice president was regional president of a national accounting association. In this capacity, the vice president had to send out a monthly newsletter and various other reports — usually on a company letterhead.

At one organization meeting of the association, Fred cornered the vice president over a cocktail. "Mr. Brown," he said, "I enjoy reading your newsletter a great deal. Where did you pick up your journalistic ability?"

"Why, thank you," Brown beamed. "But you know, writing that thing is like pulling eye teeth. It's really becoming a burden to me."

"You sure can't tell it," Fred countered. "But you know, I myself thoroughly enjoy writing."

"You *enjoy* writing?" Brown said.

"Oh, yes," Fred said. "I did a little writing for my school paper, and I still send in stuff regularly to *Accounting News.*"

Brown began to show real interest. "What have they got you doing out at the plant, Fred?"

You've no doubt guessed the outcome. Within a month, Fred was writing the newsletter and other reports for Brown. Naturally, the effort required frequent visits to Brown's office.

So how did these *associations* affect Fred's status in the organization? Well, employees in Fred's section, though envious, had to concede that Fred was "in solid" with the manager of accounting. Even more important, the manager of accounting had to acknowledge Fred's liaison with the vice president.

Thus Fred, of relatively low rank in the pecking order, has attained a degree of psychic advantage far out of proportion to his rank in the company. What about Fred's future? You've got to admit, it looks bright.

If all of this is reminiscent of a well-known Broadway play in which an office boy inveigles his way to the top by wisely selecting his *associates,* so be it. The fact remains, people judge you by your associates and your associations. If you select and nurture them with care, you can gain a degree of psychic advantage, regardless of your station.

Associating with superiors

Custom, social stratification, and organizational rigidity can all stand in the way of your being able to "associate" as freely as you might like.

For example, "subordinates" seldom fraternize with "superiors" in business and industry — and certainly not in the armed services. At college, freshmen aren't generally "accepted" by upper classmen. And in most other areas, "rookies" have got to "pay their dues" before being accepted by veterans.

Using indirect association

There are a great many instances in which you might find it necessary to gain a degree of psychic advantage by using *indirect association*. You simply align yourself with some organization or cause that is supported by the person whose favor you are trying to gain. And there are countless possibilities: the same club, the same friends, the same cafes, the same schools, the same parties, and so forth.

One bright young executive extended himself financially by negotiating a seat next to the company president's for all Dallas Cowboy games. It wasn't long before the two were talking football at the office. And it wasn't long, either, before the young man landed a promotion.

Disassociation — the other side of the coin

But what, you might ask, if your associates are *not* prestigious? What if they have a bad reputation? What does this do to your psychic advantage? The answer is, it *lessens* it, quite obviously, through *disassociation*. You lose stature in the eyes of those who judge you. This can happen on a corporate or a personal basis.

For example, several years ago, two major conglomerates were vying for what appeared to be the biggest plum on the horizon — an all-purpose, low-cost fighter plane. The project was so huge in scope that each of the two prime contractors had to select a partner for the undertaking. Since the plane was being built for both the Air Force and Navy, each prime contractor selected a partner that had had considerable experience with the Navy. Again, *association* at work.

The problem was, one of the major contractors had done its homework; the other had not. Company A selected an organization that had built thousands of Navy planes and still had a good reputation with the top Navy brass. Company B's selection, as it turned out, was not so wise. True, this subcontractor had turned out as many Navy planes as the other. But the company had, within the past few years, gotten a bad reputation for cost overruns and generally poor management.

The competition was long and intense — and razor close. Prototypes proposed by each of the two teams seemed to meet most specifications. But in the end, the Department of Defense selected Company A. Why? The Pentagon release said "superior performance possibilities and lower cost" were the determining factors. But insiders say that wasn't the case at all. Company B lost out because of its association with a contractor the Navy had lost confidence in. In other words, in all probability *disassociation* lost the cause for Company B.

This frequently happens on a personal level as well. For instance, Wilson Bradshaw, a banker, was in many respects an opposite number from Fred. He *had* the academic credentials, and most others as well. Problem was, he also had an affinity for games of chance.

Word soon got around through the rumor mill that Wilson was consorting with known gamblers. The truth is, Wilson was level-headed and played the games prudently. His "associations" with known gamblers were infrequent and casual, amounting to little more than a brief chat over a cup of coffee.

But when the chairman of the board dismissed Wilson he said, "You're known by the company you keep, and we simply can't afford to have our people associate with the people you've been seen with." In this case, Wilson would have profited by disassociation.

Association, or disassociation, can be helpful in helping you gain psychic advantage. Here's how the principle might affect a:

Junior Executive — whose wife joins a bridge club in which the boss's wife plays.

Painter — who does a portrait of a well-known celebrity and hangs it in his studio for others to see.

Salesman — who produces several letters of testimony from influential — and disinterested — third parties.

Engineer — whose by-lined article appears in a reputable trade magazine for the profession.

Professor — who makes solid affiliations with leaders in the nonacademic community.

Patience: the quiet way to gain control

We tend to equate strength with control, and appropriately so in many cases. If there's trouble in the Middle East, we send the fleet on maneuvers in the Mediterranean. Some overzealous salespeople feel they must talk their way to success — the more aggressively, the better. Many executive types feel they must perform at the top of their voices to gain and keep respect. In many cases, such tactics are undoubtedly required. This is the best way to maintain psychic advantage.

However, coming on strong isn't always the best way to keep control. In some situations there is a case — and a very strong one at that — for just the opposite approach, using infinite patience.

Playing the waiting game

Patience can result in psychic advantage to individuals in a variety of areas — from poker to politics. People who learn to play a good *waiting game* can drive their adversaries up the proverbial wall. How? Mainly by getting others to commit themselves on key issues while they hide their feelings through silence and other patient tactics.

This idea was graphically illustrated in the Korean armistice talks. American negotiators, an impetuous lot by nature, were anxious to get things over with in a hurry. The Koreans, typically patient, saw to it that the proceedings started slowly and dragged on indefinitely. Result: The Koreans attained a relatively high degree of psychic advantage. This will be discussed more fully in the chapter on being in the underdog position.

Here are two brief examples that show how individuals have learned — you might say the hard way — to gain psychic advantage.

How Joe Benson succeeded

Joe Benson is a perennial member of the life insurance industry's Million Dollar Roundtable. But things didn't always go so well for him.

Joe graduated top man in his orientation seminar. He was thoroughly prepared when he made his first call in the field. But he failed to land a sale on the first call, and the next, and the next. After the six-month probationary period, he hardly had a track record that warranted his sizeable draw.

"I was desperate," Joe said, "So finally I had a talk with my sales manager, Larry White. Larry told me to run through one of my sales presentations and he would play the role of a tough customer.

"We had a pretty stormy session, and as usual I didn't make the sale — not even in make believe. Then Larry really let me have it. 'Joe, you establish strong rapport, and you've got an excellent presentation. There's just one problem: You're too eager, and it shows.'

The danger of being too eager

"When I asked what he meant, he pointed out that I lacked the patience that a good salesman needs to help others reach a decision. For example, I had a habit of asking a closing question, such as 'Would you prefer to use your full name or only your initial on the contract?' And if the buyer did not respond immediately, I tried to keep right on selling. As Larry pointed out, the reason the buyer doesn't respond immediately is normally that he's thinking about the matter. He's trying to make up his mind. This is one of the few ways of putting legitimate pressure on the buyer. Once I developed the patience that gave the client time to think things over, my production began to increase."

Joe also learned, as many novice salesmen must learn, that the customer's first no is usually not final. Several no's can ultimately result in a yes when the salesman has the patience to let the customer make up his mind.

Joe found that *patience* was giving him a psychic advantage in sales situations that he had not enjoyed before.

Carl O'Shaughensey's case

The other case involved Carl O'Shaughensey, chief of contracts for an oil company.

"There's always a great deal of pressure put on me to negotiate new contracts as quickly as possible," Carl said. "For years I more or less yielded to that pressure. The result was that in altogether too many cases, though I did get the contract negotiated, I ended up making concessions that I shouldn't have made.

"What I came to realize was that equal, perhaps even greater, pressure was being put on the other negotiator. His company wanted *him* to get things settled as badly as ours wanted me to. Maybe more so. After all, a deadlock would probably affect them as much as, or more than, it would us."

Thus, Carl learned that in appropriate situations it's wise to play the waiting game to the hilt. Did it eventually give him psychic advantage? Listen to what happened in this incident.

"We were near the end of lengthy and often bitter negotiations with a major subcontractor," Carl said. "The subcontractor went along with just about everything at first, but belatedly began to ask for what seemed to be minor concessions, like .01 inch less tolerance on certain tooling equipment.

"My first impression was to let them have it. But I put the slide rule to their request, and it would have cost us thousands in additional set-up time.

"The subcontractor knew my management was pressing me to complete negotiations. But I happened to find out that their president was equally eager to get things settled — maybe more so. At this point, the subcontractor threatened to withdraw. However, I felt reasonably certain that this was a power play, so I felt I now really had control of the situation. As it turned out, I did, and the subcontractor signed in a few days."

The problem is, patience is something most of us don't have a great deal of. Fortunately, it is an attribute that can, through practice, be developed.

Situations where patience pays

There are many instances where patience pays off in negotiation. For example, it might well profit the:

Buyer — who takes his time filling an important order, giving sellers an opportunity to become nervous and perhaps lower their price.

Seller — who sticks to his relatively high price, even under threat of losing the business, because he realizes that the buyer really needs his particular product or service.

Poker Player — who gains the reputation of patiently waiting for an opening hand. Thus, on the infrequent occasions that he bluffs, he gains psychic advantage and maybe a sizeable pot — even though he is "negotiating" from an inferior position.

Junior Executive — who refuses to blow his stack when his boss insists on an unreasonable deadline. He realizes that after the project is completed (on schedule of course), the boss is "one down" and he is "one up."

How a buyer gains advantage

Jake Kowalski, a buyer for a large retail chain, claims that *patience*, like virtue, can be its own reward when one is dealing with a number of salespeople.

"Generally, in these situations, time is on *my* side," he says, "providing I plan ahead and get sellers to submit their bids early enough.

"Recently, for example, I sent out bids for an important order with a deadline of June 1. Actually, I didn't need the merchandise until late fall, but of course the bidders didn't know this.

Using the tactic sparingly

"I received all of the bids on or before June 1; then I sat back to play my 'waiting game.' Sure enough, the calls started coming in a couple of weeks later: 'What's the deal?' 'Where do I stand?' 'Look, I think I can improve on that bid just a little.'

"Invariably, a few of the major bidders will call in and lower their bids. I only use this tactic on special occasions, but it's an excellent way to gain psychic advantage through patience."

KEY IDEAS

Remember, a negotiation is any transaction in which one person attempts to modify the attitude or behavior of others.

You can gain a high degree of psychic advantage by mastering a wide variety of proven negotiating techniques. These include:

- *Learning to use limited authority*
  - Use the artificial limit.
  - Master the "missing man" technique.
  - Employ real or imagined authority.
- *Applying the principle of association*
  - Align yourself with the right cause.
  - Use *dis*association to advantage.
- *Using the power of patience*
  - Learn to play the "waiting game."

5

Power Tactics Used
By the Pros to Gain
Psychic Advantage

There's still much more to be learned from pros who through years of negotiating have evolved scores of successful strategies for gaining psychic advantage.

Can you use these techniques to get similar results? Undoubtedly, if you will take the time and effort required to master them. The benefits are the same — an ever-increasing control over people and situations.

In this chapter, we'll discuss a number of strategies, including:

- How to dazzle with statistics.
- Using ultimatums to gain control.
- Lowballing, highballing, and other tested techniques.

Let's discuss these in some detail.

How to dazzle with statistics

Disraeli said there are lies, damn lies, and statistics. Nowadays, there are liars, damned liars, and statisticians.

Fortunately, few recognize the validity of this statement. So this gives you a great opportunity to use statistics to maintain a high degree of control in your daily business negotiations.

If you think for a moment that a juicy statistic won't get attention, listen to conversations on street corners and around the office water cooler. For instance:

"Did you read in the *Journal* that over 50 percent of American husbands beat their wives?" one secretary said to another.

"You don't mean it," the other exclaimed. "Just as I thought, there's more of this battered wife business going on than anyone wants to admit."

Or, how about this conversation between two executives:

"I just read in the (supply your favorite publication) that the average cost of a home in Dallas is $50,000. That's bad news."

Make your figures precise

"You can say that again," the other responded. "And what makes it doubly tough is that the average income in a typical American family is now only $12,981.02 according to (supply your favorite publication). I just don't see how young people are able to buy homes nowadays."

Here's still another conversation between friends at the office:

"I think I'll switch to Virtue cigarettes. I've read that nine out of ten dentists who smoke, smoke them, so they must be good."

"What's the name of that brand again? I think I'll try 'em myself."

The art of quotesmanship

Being able to quote statistics and other facts with authority is a skill that can greatly enhance your psychic advantage over others. Fortunately, it is a skill that can be picked up rather easily.

We'll call this skill the art of *quotesmanship*. Your success in using it will depend on these factors:

1. The authority with which you speak. State your case matter of factly and press on quickly to your conclusion. This air of confidence lends credence to your quotation and discourages interruptions (such as, "Where did you get that figure?"). Your authority is further heightened if you happen to be one or more of the following: well-dressed, articulate, degreed, published, middle-aged, or in a position of authority.

2. Your ability to play on the emotions of others. Where logic and emotion are involved, the latter usually wins out. For example, the secretary who quoted the figure on "battered wives" knew she had a sympathetic listener — a woman who had actually had a few mild skirmishes with her spouse and was *willing* to believe almost any source. We'll discuss psychic advantage through listening in a later chapter.

3. The source of your information. You must be able to quote your source *as if* it were gospel. Remember, sentiment is on your side. For an adversary to refute your quote from, say, *Reader's Digest,* is almost tantamount to his questioning the Holy Bible, in the minds of many.

As a case in point, let's follow the figure quoted by Hal Ingram, the Dallas contractor who just quoted the average price of a home in Dallas as being $50,000.

Following the guidelines, he quoted the statistic from a leading national trade journal, and he did so convincingly. But how can he play on a listener's emotions with this figure? It's simple. Hal knows how to use the word *average* to *his* advantage, a prime requirement for anyone who would gain psychic advantage through *quotesmanship.*

For example, Hal sold 30 homes last year at a total sales price of $1,400,000. What is the "average" sales price? Chances are, the word *average* has one meaning for vast segments of the

American public and quite another for Hal. The public generally thinks of average as being something typical of a group, class, or series, as Webster puts it. Hal, who has done his homework, knows that technically, average is one of three things.

Three types of averages

Mean — which is obtained by adding the sales price of all homes sold and dividing by the number of homes.

Median — half of the homes sold are above this figure, the other half below it.

Mode — the sales price of the home that occurs most frequently.

In Hal's case the average sales price actually comes to three different figures: slightly over $46,666 (mean), $40,000 (median), and $30,000 (mode).

Now, here's how Hal can use this knowledge — and these different averages — to his advantage. He might tell a:

Home Buyer — "Yes, this is a rather prestigious neighborhood. The average sales price is nearly $47,000."

Tax Department — "Your appraisers ought to take another look at this area. Why, the average home here sells for only $30,000."

Public Relations Counselor — "I think you can wisely advertise this as a middle-income neighborhood. The average sales price is $40,000."

All three averages are "correct"

There you have three different averages, all "correct" in their own way. In each instance, Hal cited the average the other people wanted to hear because it best suited their needs and gave him more control over the situation.

Using an unqualified average can more often than not give you psychic advantage simply because the public is not attuned to the different meanings the term has. The media is partially responsible for this state of affairs, since they frequently use the term indiscriminately. And even when they use the term correctly, many — probably most — interpret this to mean the "average" price of a home in the "mean" sense.

Differentiating between the mean, median, and mode doesn't mean all that much where there is a reasonably narrow range between the units involved. For example, it's no doubt cricket to say that the average American male is about 5 feet, 10 inches tall. But to quote the average salary at $12,981.02 is meaningless for practical purposes. The idea again is to use the average that best suits your needs to gain a psychic advantage in the negotiation.

Other ways to use figures

In industry, for example, if you're a member of management, you'll no doubt want to use a mean average, using the board chairman's $250,000 salary to make it appear that the "average" employee is better off than he really is. And that's fine. It is, after all, an average. But as the union negotiator, you'll undoubtedly quote the mode — that is, the salary made by most employees in the company. Either of the averages is "correct." The one you will use is of course the one that will give you psychic advantage.

There is an advantage, too, in using an exact figure such as $12,981.02. In fact, the more precise the figure the better. Who can question an independent laboratory that has meticulously measured your cigarette to have only 0.02 percent tar and nicotine? Or the machine manufacturer whose lathes are designed to work to 0.00006 tolerance? How could anyone come up with a figure like that if it weren't right on the money?

The technique of "reducing to the ridiculous"

Another way to gain psychic advantage is by using what Henry Barnes, a contractor, calls "reducing to the ridiculous." For example, Henry doesn't talk too much about the cost of the home being either $65,000 or $67,000. Instead, he dwells on the difference — a mere $2,000. Reduced further, this amounts to only $18 a month, since the rule of thumb is $9 in additional house payment for every additional $1,000 in home cost. Reduced still further, that's little more than the cost of a package of cigarettes a day.

Or, let's take the mortgage banker who insists that he must charge 9.25 percent interest rather than 9 percent. "After all," he'll say, "that's only one quarter of one percent difference." He has gained an advantage over the buyer, who is still thinking in terms of a minuscule one-quarter percent. He fails to consider what that will amount to when amortized over the 30-year period of the loan.

A little can mean a lot

An astute union negotiator went one-up on his management counterpart when he negotiated for a mere additional five minutes for each break period to enable workers to get to and from the coffee machine. On an annual basis, these additional five minutes add up to thousands of lost production man-hours over a year.

Figures are funny. Analyzed and used carefully, they can contribute greatly to your psychic advantage.

Using resources resourcefully

It is important to use figures authoritatively and to play on the emotions of others, but perhaps the real key to gaining psychic advantage with statistics is to quote from what the other person considers to be a reliable source.

"Reliable sources report..."

Media reporters, who in many cases aren't allowed to divulge the source of their information, attribute their facts to all sorts of sources: "reliable sources," "Pentagon sources," "White House sources," "unimpeachable sources," or perhaps, if there's a bit of doubt, "generally reliable sources." The more credible the source, the more believable the story.

And so it is in *quotesmanship.* The more prestigious the source, the more likely you are to be believed — and to control the dialogue.

Phil Cummings, an advertising executive, plays the game of quotesmanship with a skill that often puts him on a par with — if not a few steps ahead of — the most skeptical and hard-nosed clients.

Phil's strategy is to have a wide variety of sources and then to "match" the source with the individual he's trying to go one-up on.

When trying to gain psychic advantage with a sports enthusiast, Phil will quote from *Sports Illustrated* or *The Sporting News.* With scholarly types, he'll go to *National Geographic, Atlantic Monthly,* or perhaps the *Phi Beta Kappa News.* With a business tycoon, it'll be publications like *The Wall Street Journal, U.S. News and World Report,* or perhaps a reputable trade paper or business magazine. If Phil is dealing in an area he doesn't know much about, he'll find an appropriate publication to quote from before he negotiates with the other party.

Dealing with financiers

Such was the case when Phil was attempting to negotiate a contract with a large financial house of national standing. Phil did his customary boning up for the negotiation. This gave him confidence, along with the sources from which to quote.

As Phil expected, the financier was hard-nosed and at first unflappable. But he soon began to come around under Phil's adroit display of quotesmanship.

"Well, that's all very true, Mr. Brown," Phil said in the interview, "but as I see it, FHA is planning to get back into the market. I just read in the *Kiplinger Report* that they expect to extend the amortization period on FHA loans and at the same time reduce the interest rate."

"Oh, I see you've kept up with the market," Brown scowled, trying hard not to show his delight.

Phil sensed the kill and after several more impressive quotes, closed off with, "And I wouldn't be surprised, Mr. Brown, if the legislature doesn't do something about the usury law this year. I just read in the *Congressional Report* last week that the bill is supposed to come up this month."

This time Brown couldn't mask his surprise. "Is that right," he said, "what issue was that?"

"September 30th," Phil said, "And Mr. Brown, I think we can do a tremendous PR job for you in this area."

Brown apparently agreed, for he gave Phil the account. You would have to concede that *quotesmanship* played a key role in Phil's landing the job.

The uses of "evidence"

While quoting the source may often be conclusive enough in itself, some will insist on your presenting "evidence" that what you say is true, especially in sales.

For instance, I used to quote a nationally syndicated column in the *Washington Post* as saying that real estate brokers would get eight to nine percent more for a home than an individual trying himself to sell a similar piece of property.

Some would go along with the idea after further explanation. But many, I discovered later in the survey, were skeptical because the figure did not "sound reasonable." After that, I got an original copy of the story from the *Post* and presented it as "evidence" that the statistic came from a legitimate source. The credibility factor increased substantially.

But here is where knowing the client and being able to play on his emotions entered the picture again. Showing the article to some was impressive; they recognized the *Post* as a top-ranked newspaper. Others had just the opposite reaction, disclaiming the article because they didn't trust the *Post*. And besides, "all that happened some place else."

These and many similar experiences seem to bear out the fact that executing *quotesmanship* effectively depends on your ability to size up people and situations and to apply the right quote in the right place.

To become a master at *quotesmanship*, learn to use liberally such phrases as:

"According to the *Wall Street Journal...*"

"Did you read in *The New York Times* that..."

"The Department of Labor came right out and said..."

And so forth.

Using ultimatums to gain control

"Do it or else," the neighborhood bully says.

"Or else what?" the other youngster replies.

"You'll find out," the bully says menacingly.

Eventually, of course, someone will call the bully's hand, and he'll get his comeuppance. But look at the situations he'll dominate while he's using the ultimatum, "Do it or else."

Using Boulwarism

"Take it or leave it" is one of the more frequently used ultimatum techniques, and it can be used successfully in many situations. Lemual E. Boulware, chief of labor relations for General Electric after World War II, used this method so successfully in his negotiations with unions that *Boulwarism* is a term used in modern labor relations textbooks to describe the action. Boulware worked like this.

Before starting negotiations with the unions, Boulware would get his complete wage and benefit package together. The package was generally fair and consistent with existing economic conditions. Then he would announce: "Gentlemen, we have put together a package that we feel to be fair and generous. Here it is. It represents our first and *final* offer."

True to his word, Boulware would not budge an inch on major points. And because of this firm position, union negotiators would accept his first offer, *assuming* it was being offered in good faith.

Why Boulwarism works

Why did Boulwarism work so well for so long? For a couple of reasons. First, he was a professional negotiator who had a reputation for doing his homework thoroughly and coming up with truly fair and equitable packages. Second, he stuck by his guns. When he said no changes on major issues, he meant just that. However, he *would* negotiate and frequently make concessions on minor points — a technique we'll discuss more fully in a moment.

The approach is used with more than moderate success by Frank Calhoun, an Oklahoma real estate broker. A common practice in real estate is for the seller to list his home for a few thousand dollars above its fair market value so that he can negotiate the price downward and still net the price he wants.

Working the idea in reverse

Frank reversed this trend in his office, however, by gaining the reputation for listing the property at its *actual* market value and advertising it that way. In listing sheets to other brokers, he would say, "Price firm." He was saying, in other words, "Take it or leave it." Once he created the impression that he did price homes realistically and that he did keep his word on price, other agents were reluctant to offer anything below this list price — *even when a home might have been listed at a price that was above the market value.* Thus, on occasion, "take it or leave it" definitely gives Frank a psychic advantage.

How to use fait accompli

Another closely associated ultimatum technique is what the French call *fait accompli* — the deed is done.

Carried out in good faith, or perhaps in rare instances with an ulterior motive, this strategy can be a most effective way of gaining control.

Fait accompli can be an effective strategy for giving you control and the advantage over others in important negotiations. For example, a garage owner can — and often does — legitimately use *fait accompli* to gain advantage over a customer, especially those who know little about the anatomy of an auto.

Let's say you take your car to the garage, tell the mechanic what's wrong, and ask "how much and how long?" "Hard to tell," the mechanic responds. "It could be just a loose valve, or you could need a new ring job. Drop by this afternoon, and I'll let you know."

"Good," you respond, "but you'd better let me know if it's going to be very expensive."

You return later that afternoon to find the motor dismantled and spread over the floor. "How much?" you ask.

"Around $250," the mechanic answers solemnly, adding quickly that he tried to call you three times, but the line was busy every time. So, now who has the upper hand in the negotiation? The mechanic, of course. And why? *Fait accompli,* that's why. The deed has virtually been done.

How a purchasing agent uses "deadlines"

Fait accompli sometimes works best and can swing psychic advantage to your side when it becomes apparent that the deed *had* to be done at a certain time in order to keep the operation running.

For example, Sandy Davis, purchasing agent in women's wear for a well-known Texas department store, manages somehow to make most of her really big purchases while her boss is away on business or vacation. There are a couple of reasons. Sandy knows she has better taste in women's wear than her boss does, mainly because he's ultra conservative and not attuned to contemporary fashion trends. Obviously, however, her boss holds the upper hand, since he has the final say-so on large-lot purchases. That's why Sandy buys when he's away.

Upon returning to the office and finding that Sandy has purchased a large lot of clothing, the boss insists on an explanation.

"Well, I'm sorry," Sandy will explain, "but we had to order last week to get the 20 percent discount." Or, "I had to order last week to insure shipment by fall."

How the strategy can backfire

The strategy can backfire if things don't work out. But Sandy knows her business well enough to trust her own decisions. She simply uses *fait accompli* to maintain a fairly high degree of psychic advantage over her boss.

Fait accompli is used frequently and with a high degree of success by Thomas Craft, a Houston lawyer, to give his clients psychic advantage over large companies he might be suing.

For example, he points out, many lawyers will *threaten*

to bring suit, fully anticipating that the defendant is usually more than willing to settle out of court. The bigger the company, the more likely they are to avoid the notoriety of litigation.

"This may be the thing to do in many cases," Craft pointed out. "However, I have found that *threatening* to sue can give the opposition an advantage. It might give them time to research the subject more thoroughly and to discover that they have a better case than they first thought. In such a case, the threat can backfire."

What is the advantage of suing first and then negotiating? "First, the defendant knows you mean business," Craft said. "When you take swift, decisive action it makes it appear that you have a bona fide case, whether you do or not. And if in your suit you call for quick action, it often leaves the defense without adequate time to prepare."

Deadlines can be effective

Using *fait accompli* obviously is not without risk, and besides, it doesn't always meet your needs. A somewhat similar strategy, the *deadline,* can be used just as effectively in certain situations to give you psychic advantage.

Like any strategy, a deadline must be used at the right time and in the right place to be effective. Too, the recipient of the deadline must feel the deadline is real, whether it is or not. Otherwise, it will be considered a bluff, and it might turn out to be counter-productive.

What is a *real* deadline? A newspaper deadline is real. If a reporter doesn't get his story in by a certain time, the presses will normally roll anyway. If an advertiser doesn't have his copy in by, say, a 3 p.m. cutoff time, a blank space will appear in the next edition. Advertising agencies realize this and make deadlines religiously.

Deadlines should appear real

If you can learn to use the deadline strategy effectively, and at the same time create a sense of urgency, you will have found still another solid strategem for gaining psychic advantage.

Again, the key to success is whether the deadline is real, or at least *appears* to be. Bob Andrews, purchasing agent for an oil company, has learned to use deadlines — real and imagined — to gain psychic advantage over bidders.

"This is especially true," he says, "where there are a number of bidders who are sort of spinning their wheels because there is either no deadline or only a vague cutoff date."

Giving a reason helps

It is under these circumstances that Andrews, when the strategy suits his needs, will lay down a sudden deadline. "It helps," he said, "if I give a good reason for the deadline, such as, 'I'll need your bids by this weekend, because the boss is leaving town Monday.' Or, 'I've just discovered I've got to have my answer into the corporate office by the 15th, so you'll have to have your bids in by tomorrow.'

"Using a deadline is an excellent way to get things off center," he added. "It gives me an advantage in many cases, since it sometimes forces bidders to make up their minds in a hurry, and frequently we get a break on the price under these circumstances."

Using the technique on a boss

Andrews has become so adept at the deadline technique that he can even use it on occasion to get psychic advantage over his boss. "The key," he said, "is to offer the boss a deadline that will work to *his* benefit. For example, I recently told the chief that I needed some background material and a few glossy prints by the end of the week. I quickly added that I needed all this so I could finish a magazine article on him that would appear in a leading trade publication." Did the chief meet the deadline? Yes, by two whole days.

A deadline can be a very effective way of getting another to do something by *your* timetable. You gain a psychic advantage because he is meeting the deadline under your terms, frequently forcing him to take hasty and ill-timed action.

Lowballing, highballing, and other tested tactics

Here are a few other techniques, widely used in the business world, that can be used to give you psychic advantage:

The case for lowballing

If you've bought a car, you've probably run into this situation. A dealer says, "I can give you a ball park figure of $6,000, taking your car as a trade-in." You leave to think it over. After some agonizing, you resign yourself to the $6,000 outlay and return, ready to buy.

The dealer is delighted to see you and sits down to figure out the bottom-line cost. He figures furiously, appears to become puzzled in the process, and then figures a bit more. Then with wrinkled brow, he announces solemnly: "You know, with all of the accessories you want on this car, I'm afraid it's going to cost you about $500 more than I anticipated — right at $6,500. But believe me, it's worth every penny of it." Or, "That appraiser threw me a curve. He won't allow me more than $750 on your car. Says it needs lots of work."

Why lowballing works

You're naturally upset, but you still have a psychic advantage because you can go to another dealer. Right? Usually wrong! Once you've gone through the ordeal of making a decision on *that* particular car, and once you feel you're at the *end* of the negotiating process, you tend to take the path of least resistance. So you buy. The car dealer has gained psychic advantage through lowballing.

Car dealers perhaps popularized the lowballing technique, but many others use the method, if in a more subtle fashion. For instance, Charles Thomas, a prosperous printer, realizes that most of the big jobs he'll bid on are highly competitive. Bid too high and he's out of the running. Bid too low and he loses money. So he bids relatively low to stay in the running.

Be prepared to take your lumps

Once Charley gets the bid, he ingeniously suggests ways — rather expensive ways like extra color, foldouts, and fancy layouts — to get the customer to up the ante. He thus legitimately lowballs his way to psychic advantage.

When Charley is unable to sell the "extras," he does the work at bid price and takes his lumps. But more often than not, he sells the accessories because of the esthetic qualities they add to the printing job. "I use the technique with infinite care," Charley insists, "since I'm very interested in repeat business. But once the quality of work is established, I can afford to bid a bit higher the second time around."

The opposite number: highballing

This is the other side of the coin. A seller offers his merchandise at a too-high price, planning all the while to negotiate the final price down and still net his desired profit.

Bob Wilkes, a prominent industrial Realtor, gains psychic advantage differently from the way Frank Calhoun, the Oklahoma Realtor, does. Calhoun, you'll recall, gained advantage by establishing a "firm" price. Wilkes does just the opposite, starting with an obviously high figure and then selling at a lower figure, which is nearer the fair market value anyway. The technique is suitable to big-ticket commercial property, which is hard to price in the first place.

For example, Bob once listed for sale a downtown building in Denver. Before he had the property appraised, he quoted a sales price of $2.3 million (which he suspected to be slightly above the real value) to an interested buyer. The buyer, who was itching to make the purchase, deliberated several days over the project. Finally, he came back with a "firm offer" of $2 million.

Raising the "ante"

"Sorry," Bob said, "but I've had some informal talks with a few industrial appraisers, and unofficially they're thinking in terms of $2.5 million. The property's apparently worth more than I thought."

"Look," the buyer said heatedly, forgetting his $2 million low offer. "Now a deal's a deal. How about it?"

"Well," Bob said, "I suppose you've got a point. A deal *is* a deal. Let's draw up the papers."

Highballing obviously gave Bob the psychic advantage, since the buyer felt "lucky" to get the overpriced property for $2.3 million. This is exactly what Bob had in mind all along.

Lowballing and highballing go on all the time. You can definitely gain psychic advantage by learning to use these techniques expertly.

Mixing apples and oranges

One of the surest ways of gaining psychic advantage over others is to create a high state of confusion. And one effective

way to do this is to have someone compare dissimilar objects —
like the proverbial apples and oranges.

The first step is to give vague orders or ambiguous
specifications. Then when it comes time to make a decision,
you can "interpret" the order to your advantage.

It can happen at high levels of government. For example,
some years ago, Secretary of Defense Robert McNamara sent
out bids for an all-purpose, variable-wing fighter plane that
could be used by both the Air Force and the Navy. Primary attention would be paid to cost, performance, and a new factor
— commonality, which meant that the planes should have as
many common parts as possible so that it could be made
cheaper.

After lengthy and sometimes bitter negotiations, a
government selection team chose the Boeing entry because it
was cheaper and could fly faster and farther with a bigger
bomb load. But McNamara reversed the decision in favor of
the General Dynamics version, which he claimed had more
commonality.

Decision-makers thus had to evaluate the higher commonality of the General Dynamics version (apples) with the
performance and cost advantage of Boeing's plane (oranges).
How do you equate the two? Only McNamara had the answer.
The answer, which followed a long and bitter congressional
investigation, turned out to be commonality.

Tommy Umbarger, a purchasing agent, sometimes uses
the apples-and-oranges technique to gain psychic advantage
over bidders.

"I try to write specifications in the broadest possible
terms," he said. "This leaves room for some interpretation —
and yes, some creativity — by bidders. For example, we might
leave the type of material or the color or the weight of the
product to the bidder's discretion. Then when we get our bids,
we can weigh these factors in our own mind and reach a de-

cision based on *our* interpretation of the specs. It gives us an advantage and at the same time enables us to keep the good will of most of our bidders."

Making concessions

Negotiation is a give-and-take process. You win a point here, concede a point there. It is the art of making these concessions that determines how successfully you negotiate.

Basically, you can gain psychic advantage in making concessions by following these two guidelines:

1. Don't make a concession simply because the other party makes one.
2. Swap minor concessions for a major one, if possible.

Let's discuss these points briefly.

Returning a favor is natural

We are generally programmed to treat others fairly. Hence the strong tendency to return a favor when the other party grants one, to concede a point when another makes a concession.

Naturally, many situations will call for just this kind of reciprocity. For example, if a buyer agrees to buy an extra-large lot of merchandise, the seller has no alternative than to bring his price down. But there are other instances where it is possible to gain psychic advantage by not returning the concession, as Mark Simms, a top-flight insurance adjuster, has discovered.

"For example," he said, "I've had claimants argue long and loud with me on their claims, only to finally relent and say,

'Look, I want to be fair about this. I'm willing to lower my claim to only $5,000 if you folks will be fair with me.'

"I've found that in many such cases, when people make this kind of concession, they are doing so out of frustration, or maybe even desperation. I've discovered that I can gain control of the situation in many of these cases by *not* reciprocating. Instead, the idea is to question the validity of their claim in the first place.

"For instance, a Houston family put in a rather heavy fire damage claim on their home. I investigated and recommended to the company that we settle for only $750 — an amount considerably below their claim. After lengthy discussion, they finally conceded that they would lower the claim to include just the kitchen and dining areas, a major concession on their part. Instead of returning the concession, I began to question the validity of the claim in the first place. I questioned how such a fire could be limited to just the kitchen and the living area and not spread further. I implied, in other words, that there was some skulduggery going on, and there probably was. Before I left, the family was glad to accept my check for $750, which was the figure I had hoped to pay all along. In this case, I definitely gained control by not returning the concession."

Swapping concessions

Being able to swap minor concessions for major ones is a technique that every successful negotiator should master. Wives are sometimes masters of this technique, as attested by this conversation between Sam and Gloria. They're discussing the family budget.

"Look, we can cut lots of corners if you want," Gloria said, "but we've either got to add a fourth bedroom or buy a bigger house."

"We've been through this before," Sam said, "and we can't afford it just now."

"I've controlled the budget for 19 years," Gloria said, "and trust me, we *can* afford it."

"But it'll put us in too much of a bind," Sam said. "Look, I need some new clothes."

"Charge them," Gloria said, "I'll put it in the budget."

"I don't know where the money's coming from," Sam countered. "Besides, you know I've already committed myself to joining the new tennis club. *That's* business."

"I know," Gloria said, "and I've made provisions in the budget for that, too."

"Well, okay," Sam said, "but I guess I can just forget that new fishing tackle I wanted."

"No, I want you to have fun on your fishing trips," Gloria said. "It's good for your mental health."

What is the box score on this negotiation? Gloria: three minor concessions totalling about $1,000. Sam: a new house costing Lord knows what.

Gloria not only successfully swapped minor concessions for a major one, she also used another technique commonly employed by skilled negotiators. She listed at the outset one item — the new bedroom — which was non-negotiable. Strange how often others will accept such "untouchable" items without question. Like the deadline, the other party tends to accept it as theirs.

Negotiating the "non-negotiable"

Bob Ambrose, a successful lawyer, tries to use the non-negotiable technique, whether he is trying a divorce case or negotiating a contract for a client.

"Generally," he says, "I try to pick an issue or item that

appears to be of little or only marginal value to my client. This makes the request seem fair and plausible to my opponent."

New "use" for furniture

For example, Ambrose once represented a lady seeking a divorce. As part of the settlement, he asked for an "even distribution of all assets," including money and property.

"However," he said in the negotiation with the other party, "there's one thing my client insists on — the furniture. She spent a lot of time and effort in buying most of it. Naturally, she has become emotionally attached to it. Therefore, we'll be willing to consider a trade-off; say, giving your client the third car and giving mine the furniture. But she insists on keeping the furniture; it's one point on which we can't negotiate."

"Well," the opposing attorney says, "I see no particular problem there. I think I can go ahead and agree on this point."

Gaining the objective

Ambrose has thus gained a clear psychic advantage, mainly because he has done his homework. Many of the pieces of furniture bought by his client were antiques — some very valuable. The furniture was perhaps worth ten times the value of the car.

The actual negotiations got heated. Issues became confused, and at one point the opposing attorney said, "All right, let's avoid all of this hassle and just split things down the middle."

"Hold on," Ambrose responded. "Don't forget, my client gets the furniture. We agreed on it."

"All right," the opposing attorney agreed begrudgingly. We did make a deal — the furniture for the car. But everything else goes right down the middle."

Negotiating a contract

In this case, the furniture-for-car swap met the basic requirements for using a non-negotiable item. The request seemed plausible and appeared to be of minor importance. In reality, Ambrose had researched the issue thoroughly and knew the value of the furniture.

In another case, Ambrose was negotiating a contract for a major aerospace contractor with a subcontractor for production of some high-priority parts.

Ambrose was flexible on almost all items except one: His client, he said, insisted that the subcontractor allow the prime contractor to have an inspector on the subcontractor's premises to approve parts before shipment.

Meeting the requirements

Again, the request seemed innocuous enough. But again, Ambrose had done his homework. The parts, he discovered in his research, were to be made to especially tight tolerances that would require the latest — and most expensive — equipment.

Later, in the negotiation, when the subcontractor realized the complexity of the task, it sought to alter the agreement. But the item, you'll recall, was non-negotiable.

The non-negotiable item should be meaningful *to you.* If it meets this basic requirement, it can give you considerable psychic advantage in negotiations.

KEY IDEAS

Professional negotiators use a variety of tactics to gain the upper hand. You'll need to master these tactics yourself in order to constantly gain a high degree of psychic advantage. They include:

- *Dazzling with statistics*
  - Develop the art of quotesmanship.
  - Use statistics authoritatively.
  - Cultivate reliable sources.
  - Present "evidence."
- *Using ultimatums to gain control*
  - Practice the take-it-or-leave-it technique.
  - Perfect the *fait accompli* technique.
  - Use deadlines for effect.
  - Make concessions on minor points.
- *Lowballing, highballing, and other tested techniques*
  - Mix apples and oranges.
  - Stress non-negotiable items.

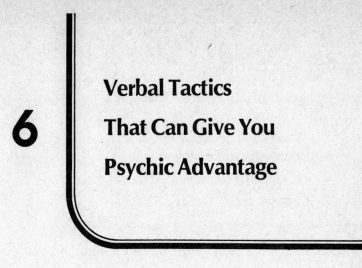

6

Verbal Tactics That Can Give You Psychic Advantage

As Emerson pointed out so concisely, you are what you *say*. Your conversation is your "signature," the yardstick by which others constantly judge you. It can also be one of your most potent weapons in your continuing quest for psychic advantage.

Give more than you take

Good conversation should be give-and-take. And normally, you should give more than you take in order to gain psychic advantage. But not always! The main idea in having psychic advantage is to *control* the thrust of the conversation, not necessarily to dominate it. After all, you rarely "win" by intimidating the other party.

To gain psychic advantage, you'll need to perfect effective ways to guide the conversation into channels that will benefit you, to control the conversation when it's to your advantage to do so, and to make the other person *want* to cooperate and, in the process, give you the psychic advantage you seek.

Benefits to be gained

By mastering effective verbal tactics, you can become:

- A dominant force in business
- A masterful negotiator
- A sought-after conference leader
- A magnetic personality

You can do all these things by becoming adept at:

- Exploring for conversational clues
- Controlling the conversation
- Talking like an expert

Let's discuss each of these.

Exploring for conversational clues

"John," Betty inquired, "do you think my eyes sparkle like stars?"

"Yep," John replied.

"And are my lips as luscious as honey melon?"

"Yep."

"And is my hair as silky as satin?"

"Yep."

"And is my complexion as soft as velvet?"

"Yep."

"Oh, John, you're such a wonderful conversationalist!"

Marriage results

This type of scintillating "conversation" gained John psychic advantage over Betty in the form of her hand in marriage. Which illustrates an important point: You don't always have to strictly *talk* your way to psychic advantage. *Active* listening, followed by effective conversation, can turn the trick if you can determine the other person's basic needs and problems.

Determining needs and problems

In conversation, gaining psychic advantage translates roughly into "getting your way." And it stands to reason, the other person is never more willing to let you have your way than when you understand and show interest in his basic needs and problems.

Thus an effective way of gaining verbal psychic advantage is to: 1) listen actively; 2) determine the other's basic needs and problems; 3) use this information to gain your objective.

Listen to this brief conversation between a salesman and a new owner of a condominium. The owner would normally have initial psychic advantage since he has the power to buy or not buy the home-protection system the salesman is trying to sell.

"Winning" at conversation

Salesman: Good evening. Thanks for giving me a few minutes of your time.

Prospect: No problem. But I do have some things to do. And as I told you over the phone, I'm really satisfied with the protection the condominium people give us.

Salesman: I understand. Incidentally, that's an interesting picture you have over your fireplace. Did you fly P-51s in the war?

Prospect: Oh, that. No, not actually. That is, yes, I did fly in the "big war," but it was in P-38s, not P-51s. I

fly the old Mustang now as a member of the Confederate
Air Force. In fact, that picture was taken only last month.

Salesman: Confederate Air Force...Oh, yes, that's
the group of W.W. II pilots who collect old planes, fix
'em up, and fly 'em in air shows, isn't it?

Prospect: Right. I guess we're now flying just
about every major fighter and bomber flown in W.W. II,
and that includes both Allied *and* German planes.

Salesman: Including the old "Flying Coffin"?

Prospect: The old B-25? Yeah, sure, we've got one
of them, too. How did you know about that old bird?

Salesman: Well, I ought to. I mean, I flew 25
missions in them! Not a bad plane, really.

Prospect: In Europe?

Salesman: No. Well, yes, I mean...from Italy.

Prospect: When were you in?

Salesman: Well, I stayed in. Actually, I just retired
from the military as a colonel a few years ago.

Prospect: Retired, huh. Say, that's great. You know,
I've been in the reserves all the while, and I'll be retiring
from that shortly. But I won't get nearly the retirement
pay you do. You know, at one time, I thought seriously
about staying in after the big one.

Salesman: Really?

Prospect: Yeah, you know I *love* to fly. And let's
face it, the service offered a lot of security. Just think,
if I had stayed in, I could be retired on three-quarters pay
right now.

Salesman: Well, I enjoyed the service. Incidentally,
what are you doing now?

Prospect: Oh, I'm working for the city.

Salesman: Good place to work, I understand.

Prospect: Not bad. Like every place, it's got its
good points and its bad points. But that's immaterial, because I'm locked in anyway.

Salesman: Locked in?

Prospect: Yeah. I'm about 80 percent vested in the savings and retirement plan. And if I can stick it out for 10 more years, I can retire at two-thirds pay.

Salesman: Sounds great.

Prospect: Well, it is. Except that it knocked me out of a chance to make a bundle.

Salesman: How's that?

Prospect: Well, my wife's uncle gave us a chance to buy in on a regional distributorship he owns part of.

Salesman: Sounds like a ground-floor opportunity.

Prospect: It was...I guess still is. But we'd have to take almost all of our money out of savings and plunk it down. The risk isn't really all that great. But boy, what if things went wrong?

Salesman: I see what you mean.

Remarks tell the tale

By conversationally exploring for clues, the salesman was able to detect the prospect's strong need for safety and security. This is reflected in his remarks about the service and his reluctance to enter into a potentially lucrative business transaction.

Having uncovered this clue, the salesman is now prepared to gain psychic advantage by dramatizing the fail-safe protection afforded by his system.

Is this manipulation?

But, you say, isn't this manipulation? Not really. I think most salesmen will agree that to sell a person something against their will, something they don't basically need and want, is manipulative. But to sell them something they genuinely need and desire, something that is in their best interests, is the true essence of persuasion. It is manipulative only to the extent that you discovered the need that's there and intensified the desire.

The salesman gains psychic advantage, all right. But he gains it fair and square.

Security and safety are basic needs, along with the need to belong, sometimes called the social need. Then there are the needs involving self-esteem and self-actualization. We all have these needs, and the problems they create from time to time. The idea in gaining conversational psychic advantage is to find out what these needs and problems are. The obvious way is through active listening and effective conversation.

How Jan got her typewriter

For example, Jan Flanagan, a new secretary on the job, had developed a strong propensity for a typewriter with script type. She requested one from her new boss.

"They cost too much," he said, "And besides, they don't impress me all that much." That ended that.

But within a few months, Jan knew her boss a lot better, and this time, she used a different approach.

Self-esteem is the answer

"You no doubt remember the script typewriter I mentioned a few months ago," she said. "Well, the new models do an even more outstanding job. For example, here's a copy of a personal letter our board chairman sent to the mayor on his secretary's script typewriter. And here's one to our president from the head of our ad agency — script type again. And here's another one from..."

"Wait! Hold On," the boss interrupted. "I get the point. You're right; it does look great. Get one."

Jan gained a good deal of psychic advantage in this and other negotiations with her boss by recognizing his very strong need for *self-esteem*.

Other needs cited

The social need is often manifested by a desire to talk a great deal. It is possible in these cases to gain control by letting the other person actually do most of the talking. This is true, of course, only so long as you are seeking conversational clues with which you can help that person solve his problems.

Self-actualization, which means living up to the best within yourself, is one of the strongest human needs at the higher level. This one can be used in most business and professional environments, and in homes as well, as demonstrated by Robert Harper.

How marriage is helped

Harper admits to gaining "much greater control" in his marriage after realizing that his wife's discontent could be traced to her inability to use her basic talents.

"Frances had a degree in interior design," he said, "but we got married and started raising our family right after college. As a result, she never really had a chance to use it.

"But after the kids got out of college, she became more restless and dissatisfied. That's when we talked it over and decided that she ought to go back to work and use this talent. She did, and I'm master of the house once again. Thank goodness!"

People don't walk around with a sign on their chest advertising their *needs*. But the signs are there — conversationally, that is — if you'll only take the time and trouble to look for them.

Key techniques for controlling the conversation

While you'll constantly want to listen actively in order to ferret out the other person's needs and problems, there are times when you will want to control the conversation yourself.

One way to gain control is to *lead* the other person, gently but firmly, toward *your* predetermined goals. This should be done more by design than by accident, and this means planning.

For example, Mark Cravens, a commercial real estate operative, is attending a social event. His goal is to seek out Rod Thompson, president of a New Jersey firm that is moving to Houston. It has been rumored that the New Jersey firm is to merge with a Houston company.

Knowing this, Mark meets Thompson and strikes up this conversation:

Making a point

Mark: I've read about your move to Houston, Mr. Thompson. I suppose most of your top people are coming with you.

Thompson: I'm not sure right now just how many will make the move.

Mark: I see. Well, that's quite a transition to make — New Jersey to the sun belt, and Houston at that.

Thompson: No doubt about that.

Mark: I know it's not an easy job. Real estate's awfully high in the areas where *your* executives will likely want to live. At least, that's what Mr. Pearson found out.

> Thompson: Pearson?
>
> Mark: Yes, Rodney Pearson, president of Allied Industries.
>
> Thompson: I know who he is. But how did you get hooked up with him?
>
> Mark: Well, Mr. Thompson, mergers *are* my specialty, and here's how it happened...

Mark now has the floor, and potentially, psychic advantage — all by design. He's gaining control because he's talking to the other person's interests and holding forth in an area of his expertise.

It's almost always more effective to *show* a person how competent you are than to tell them. And this is precisely what Mark has done in leading the conversation toward *his* objectives.

Careful planning and conversational expertise are the key ingredients here.

Leading with a question

One effective way to lead the other person toward *your* predetermined goal is by asking the right question at the right time, and of course, in the right way. We will explore the process of gaining psychic advantage through effective questioning fully in a later chapter.

Briefly, however, let's take a look at how questions can be used to steer the conversation toward a desired goal, with psychic advantage in mind.

Tess Brownlee, Realtor

Let's assume, for example, that Tess Brownlee, a real estate saleslady, has carefully qualified her prospect and shown him a home that seems to suit his every need. He seems

very interested, but in the final analysis wants to "think it over."
At this point, the prospect obviously assumes psychic advantage, since he's the only one who knows precisely what it is that
needs to be thought over. He will maintain this advantage so
long as he keeps this information to himself.

But notice how Tess, a skilled interviewer, *leads* the
client to an answer that suits her needs and puts her on the
track toward regaining the psychic advantage that she had
momentarily lost.

Questions, questions, questions

> **Tess:** I can understand your wanting to think it
over, Mr. Jones. It *is* a big decision. But do you mind my
asking, is it the location you're unhappy with?
> **Prospect:** No. No, it's not the location at all. This is
the part of town we had in mind.
> **Tess:** Is it the price?
> **Prospect:** Well, it is a little steep. But no, I think
we can swing the price all right.
> **Tess:** How about the school district, Mr. Jones?
You were quite concerned with that. Does it meet your
requirements?
> **Prospect:** It's fine. No problem there.
> **Tess:** Well, Mr. Jones, how about the monthly pay-
ment? Does that bother you? I know we've gone beyond
the figure you originally mentioned.
> **Prospect:** The monthly payment...well, frankly, it
is a little higher than we expected to pay. We could make
it, all right, but it might pose somewhat of a problem for
the time being...

How Tess takes over

Mission accomplished! Tess now has a chance to regain
psychic advantage. As a pro, she can perhaps cope with "the

monthly payment is too much" because she knows how to attack the problem. But very few are able to get a handle on "I want to think it over."

Tess was successful in getting the information she wanted because she had become an expert in the rather ancient art of asking skillful questions aimed at leading the other person to a precise answer. It can be a highly effective way of gaining psychic advantage through strong verbal tactics.

Passing the verbal buck

People who become very skilled at gaining psychic advantage learn to lead a general conversation in such a way as to make *them* look good, even at someone else's expense.

For example, let's assume you're on a coffee break with coworkers. You're anxious because you have to buy a new car. The reason you're having to buy a new car is because of a new personnel policy set by Al Paxton, the personnel director, who also happens to be your competition for a top spot in the company.

Avoid "sour grapes"

Now, for you to come right out and criticize Al and his new policy would appear to be sour grapes. But you can avoid this by *leading* the conversation to the issue itself and then letting someone else do the actual criticizing.

A leading statement might be: "Boy, I'm confused. I've looked at four new cars and I just can't make up my mind."

After a brief discussion in this vein, someone asks: "Buying a new car, huh? What's the matter, your old car giving out on you?"

"No, it's not that," you reply amiably. "I guess since we can't take company cars home any more, we just have to have another one in the family."

What to do when the subject is in the open

Now the subject is in the open. Remember, it is Al Paxton, the personnel director, who has decreed that company cars can't be taken home and used privately. Obviously, the new policy is unpopular.

"You know," one member of the group mentions, "I never had too much use for that Al Paxton anyway. Not since he cut out unlimited per diem on trips."

Coming to the defense

You do *not* agree, of course. In fact, in an effort to enhance your good-guy role, you *defend* Paxton's position. "Now, let's not be too rough on Al. After all, you know, he's got his problems, too. He *must* have a valid reason for taking our cars away like he did!"

"Like what?" someone asks.

At this point, you merely shrug your shoulders as if to say, "Beats me."

Mission accomplished

Others will continue to berate Paxton in no uncertain terms. They emerge as the "heavies." But you have come out on top as the good guy. You even *defended* Al. You've controlled the situation beautifully.

Again, the idea is to lead people to the conclusion you want them to reach, and in the process to gain psychic advantage.

Keeping "cool" is a factor

It should go without saying that you can't very well control a conversation — nor the people in it — unless you can control yourself and your temper. It should, but it doesn't. There are plenty of people, like Bob Woodruff, who have acquired a high degree of psychic advantage, but only after learning how to control their anger.

"I used to think I could get mad, stomp my feet, and get my way," Bob said. "What I didn't realize was that the more I did this, the more I lost control of the situation. There's no doubt in my mind. You can gain an appreciable degree of control over many situations simply by suppressing your anger and keeping your cool.

Following a formula

Bob's formula for gaining psychic advantage through anger control is:

1. If time permits, work the anger off. Talk it out in the next room or while driving home.

2. Prepare yourself for outbursts by analyzing what causes them. Describe the precise feelings this anger causes and the effect it has on your relations with others.

3. If you can't avoid anger, *tell* the other person about it, calmly and unemotionally. This tends to put things up front and lessens the chances of your showing extreme anger.

Talking like an expert

Previously, we asserted that psychic advantage is frequently gained through *legitimacy*. People tend to place great stock in diplomas, certificates, testimonials, almost anything that has a "legal" appearance.

But all of these items are things you can *see*. The question here is, can you gain the same sort of advantage with the spoken word?

I think you can. It's simply a matter of learning to talk like an expert. Adding "verbal legitimacy" to your repertoire can add immeasurably to your ability to gain psychic advantage.

How to talk a good game

How do you *talk* like an expert? You use the language of one who is steeped in the business or profession. In other words, you "talk *their* language."

This entails, at a minimum, a basic understanding of the area of expertise under consideration and, just as importantly, the ability to learn and use the jargon of that business or profession.

And how do you accomplish these goals? It takes research — plain old digging for the facts.

How Joyce Brothers did it

Joyce Brothers, the nationally syndicated psychologist, proved the point some years ago in the popular "$64,000 Question" television program. She won top dollar by answering questions about boxing that would have baffled sports writers and genuine boxing buffs of long standing.

Was Joyce Brothers a bona fide boxing expert? Not in the least. She hadn't seen over a couple of fights in her life. She learned all about the sport by virtually "memorizing" the encyclopedia of boxing over a several-month span. But to the public, she was an expert.

Becoming an "instant expert"

Indeed, you can become an expert and maintain a high degree of control and psychic advantage by "boning up" on your appropriate subject.

For example, if you're planning to see a lawyer about a will, read up on the subject beforehand. If you're going to see a doctor, find out what your medical manual says about your ailment.

Holding your own

You won't, of course, become a bona fide expert. But you can assimilate at least enough to "talk a good game." If you don't gain psychic advantage, you at least gain a degree of parity in your transaction with these experts.

But doctors and lawyers are members of the "learned professions." With them, the idea is to pick up just enough knowledge to hold your own.

With most others, the idea is to learn enough to actually give you the psychic advantage.

Selling an idea

For example, I once was in the position of having to sell a course on "Personal Goal Setting" to a committee comprised mainly of educators, including several psychologists. The course was to be aimed at predominantly adult groups.

My degree is not in psychology, though as a training consultant I have had wide exposure to the discipline. Still, psychologists and educators tend to look askance at anyone who does not have advanced *formal* training in their discipline. On paper, the committee definitely had psychic advantage.

Doing the homework

How did I overcome this "disadvantage"? By doing my homework.

I read several books by leading authorities on "career-pathing," as behavioral psychologists and personnel experts call it. I boned up on the leading aptitude tests and even exposed myself to Johnson O'Connor's Human Engineering Laboratory — one of the most sophisticated institutions for measuring human aptitudes.

Talking "their" language

I had learned the lingo, so to speak, and I used it liberally at my meeting with the committee. The committee was aware of my general educational experience and background, but halfway through the meeting, I had gained "acceptance." We were all talking the language of the "fraternity."

This went a long way toward my winning the contract. But it seemed to me that what really clinched the deal was the "evidence" of my expertise that I brought along with me, a copy of my cassette program on goal-setting and a magazine article on the same subject. These, in my opinion, are what tilted the psychic advantage in my direction.

Opposites do attract

It seems that everybody envies the other person. Business executives tend to hold well-known members of the academic world in awe, probably because of the guilt feelings they have about the "tunnel vision" they have developed in their own specialty. Academicians, on the other hand, tend to defer to the hard-nosed pragmatist who has "made it" in the business world.

If you can learn the lingo and then write a book or article or give a speech on the subject, you're on your way to true psychic advantage with almost any group.

Words can make a difference

The words you use to get your message across can go a long way toward helping you gain psychic advantage.

As already shown, it's helpful to use the language of the expert when dealing with the expert.

For example, with financial people, throw in terms like *leaseback, capitalization ratios,* and *wraparound loans* as if they had always been a part of your working vocabulary. With lawyers, toss in an occasional *habeas corpus, nolo contendere,* or the like. And so forth. This technique can be carried out with considerable verve if you will just do your homework.

Using "fact" vs. "feel" words

But it is the choice of rather common words that can make the big difference.

Some words cause us to think rationally; others cause us to react emotionally. The *situation* will dictate which to use in your quest for psychic advantage.

For example, in general real estate, salespeople frequently tell an owner they'll be glad to try to sell their *house.* On the other hand, they invariably try to sell buyers a *home.*

There is a difference

The two words do conjure up different mental pictures. A *house,* after all, is just another structure — brick, wood, and mortar. But a *home* is something your kids will grow up in. It's "where the heart is." It is a highly emotional word designed to give salespeople psychic advantage in getting top dollar.

Precisely how and where you will want to use emotional words depends entirely on your own situation, and of course the circumstances.

Ask how they feel

I like emotional words in selling because they cause people to buy. That's why as a sales manager I spent some time getting my people to use words that stress emotions. They were told never to ask a prospect what he *thinks* about a product; rather, they were to ask them how they *feel* about it.

Not that "fact" words don't have their place. When locked in debate with someone who is overpowering me with expertise or dazzling me with professional jargon, I retaliate with such rarely used words as *vicissitudes, pusillanimous, contretemps, indefatigable,* and *anachronistic.*

These are what I call "stopper words" — words that your adversary is not likely to instantly comprehend. But since he's regaling you with his own high-flown language, he's not about to admit his ignorance. Result: You're on your way to gaining psychic advantage.

Talking like a winner

I have found that there is still another way to win with words in the business world. You learn to use the pet words of "winners" in the organization.

For example, I once knew a highly articulate division manager who liked to play with words. One month it would be "parameters," the next month "visibility," the next month "value structure," and so forth. He used the words expertly.

I observed that virtually every top expert in the company, or every person who aspired to a top spot, would start using the division manager's pet phrases and words.

How parroting pays off

I am almost positive that such parroting paid off. Practically every person who went up in the organization played the manager's word game. You might say, the ability to perk up and parrot pet phrases gave them psychic advantage.

Why is this? Because people generally like to hear "their" words and ideas played back to them. Emulation is still apparently one of the highest types of praise.

Getting to your subject

Of course, to talk like an expert, you have to discourse on a subject that you're steeped in. The problem is in finding ways to get to that subject.

One obvious way is to simply take the initiative yourself and broach the subject.

Dan Fisher, for example, is a self-styled expert on three subjects: politics, football, and the stock market.

Regardless of the nature of the conversation, he'll eventually get around to one of these topics, at which point he gains psychic advantage in most conversations.

Perhaps a slightly more realistic approach to putting yourself in the verbal spotlight is to "question" your way there. The idea is for you to know the answer (and know it well) before asking the question.

How Rod Hillburn uses the technique

Rod Hillburn, a personnel generalist, resorts to this technique often, especially when he is the "underdog" in the transaction.

For example, Rod found himself being almost constantly intimidated by his firm's director of contracts, who was a lawyer. There were two primary reasons for the tension — the lawyer's status and his disdain for "personnel people." One day, Rod "attacked."

"Why is it," he asked the lawyer, "that we can't even ask a person's age, sex, or marital status on an employment application these days without getting into trouble?"

"What's that?" the lawyer responded. "What do you mean? I see nothing wrong with that. In fact, I hardly see how you could do your job without asking these questions."

"No, it's for real," Rod continued. "It's the new government ruling, and I'm afraid there are more restrictions to come."

"You don't say," the director said. "Like what?"

Rod then proceeded to unleash his encyclopedic knowledge of the government's Equal Employment Opportunity Act. The lawyer listened intently, showing almost admiration of Rod's ability to expound on the legalistic aspect of the act.

How Rod gains "advantage"

Did Rod gain a degree of psychic advantage? You bet. And he did so by following the formula to the letter.

First, the question was phrased in a professional manner. Second, Rod knew the answer well, since he had just attended a seminar on the subject. Third, he was certain the lawyer didn't know the answer because the subject was a relatively "new" one and Rod had tested the water, so to speak, with a few "trial questions."

A well-phrased question, properly executed, can put you on the road to psychic advantage. It's another verbal tactic you'll want to master.

Rules of the "game"

The game can be played in either a big or small group. The requirements are: 1) the question *sounds* professional;

2) you know the answer well; 3) the other party does *not* know the answer or doesn't know it nearly as well as you do. The purpose of the game, of course, is to impress others and at the same time gain a degree of psychic advantage.

Quizzing the official

For example, in a head-on interview with a company official, you might pose a tough question such as, "If the new energy bill passes, won't that force us to redesign our power system?"

"Could be," the official says, "but I really don't know enough to make that kind of evaluation."

That's just what you wanted to hear. Now you can strut your stuff — and gain psychic advantage in the process.

KEY IDEAS

Being able to guide and control conversation is a prerequisite to gaining a high degree of psychic advantage.

You can gain the advantage by:

- *Exploring for conversational clues*
  - Learn how to guide the conversation.
  - Determine others' needs and problems.
  - Satisfy their needs.
- *Controlling the conversation*
  - Guide *him* to *your* goal.
  - Lead with solid questions.
  - Pass the verbal buck.
  - Keep your cool.

- *Talking like an expert*
  - Talk *their* language.
  - Become a jargon expert.
  - Talk like a winner.

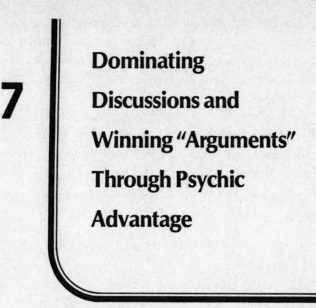

7

Dominating Discussions and Winning "Arguments" Through Psychic Advantage

Obviously, one of the most effective ways to gain Psychic Advantage over others is by "outtalking" them, by "winning" the discussion.

But there's the rub. You rarely "win" an argument, even when you dazzle your opponent with logic and oratorical prowess. In fact, in many cases, the more brilliant your argument, the less likely you are to change another's position or frame of mind.

Persuasion is the answer

For instance, back in school, I used to love to debate. I found it exciting, challenging, and mentally stimulating. Not that I was that good, mind you; as I recall it, I easily lost as many debates as I won.

But even when I lost, I noticed something rather strange.

151

I never really *felt* that I had lost. I accepted the fact that the decision went against me, all right, but deep down I really didn't accept the loss. And now that I think back, I'm fairly certain that my opponents were just as reluctant to accept an adverse decision.

A few years later, something quite similar happened in selling. I would "overwhelm" my prospect with a fail-proof plan and irrefutable logic, yet in altogether too many cases, fail to make the sale.

Losing the "war"

In both cases, it was a case of winning the battle but losing the war.

And this is precisely the point to remember in gaining psychic advantage. The idea is to win, but in such a manner that the other party does not *feel* defeated. This causes resentment and usually precludes your being able to gain true psychic advantage.

And how do you do this? Basically, by remembering that people are usually convinced more by emotion than by logic. This doesn't, of course, mean that you should not build a strong "factual" presentation. It simply means that when it comes to changing another's way of thinking, you are more likely to succeed by giving them an "emotional" reason and by giving them a chance to "save face" when you do win.

An idea worth remembering

This is an idea worth etching into your memory. The next step is to master proven techniques that will enable you to persuade others to your point of view.

Generally, there are three steps involved in the art of persuading so that you end up with clear psychic advantage.

They are:

1. *Get the other person to abandon his point of view.* And remember he, like you, is inclined to cling to his ideas tenaciously, no matter how irrational they might be.
2. *Get him to accept your point of view.* This often includes his accepting *you* as well as the ideas you represent.
3. *Allow him to save face.* Whoever said he'd rather be right than president apparently articulated a universal human longing. The other side of the coin is that most people will accept defeat more gracefully if they aren't made to "look bad" in the process. A person convinced against his will is still of the same opinion.

How to reach your goals

Keeping these basic principles in mind, let's explore some basic steps for increasing your psychic advantage in discussions with others. Learn to:

- Interpret opposition as interest.
- Disagree gracefully and let the other person save face.
- Dramatize key points and thoughts.
- Minimize irrational behavior.

Interpret opposition as interest

Harry Wright became a successful insurance salesman, but only after changing his way of thinking 180 degrees. He confessed to being a "failure" during the early part of his career simply because he was taking prospects literally when they said no.

Nowadays, Harry is usually encouraged when people say no. He has come to realize that, generally speaking, a prospect is usually "interested" only when he shows some form of resistance. "I get concerned when they offer no resistance at all," Harry said, "when they're *too* agreeable."

Resistance indicates a void

"Obviously, people do sometimes mean it when they give you a negative response. But I'd say that nine times out of ten, some form of resistance is a good sign. When a prospect begins to ask questions and raise objections, this gives me something to work on. He's telling me that there's a void within himself, that he's internally waging a debate over what to do.

"Again, it's when he's totally indifferent, when he doesn't ask questions or raise objections, that I anticipate having a real problem of persuading him to my point of view."

Harry interviews Art

Let's listen in briefly to this dialogue between Harry and a prospect we'll call Art.

Harry: Art, I'd certainly like to see you upgrade your insurance program. You know, based on your present income, you ought to be carrying at least ten times more life insurance to adequately take care of your family if something were to happen to you."

Art: Yeah. I know.

Harry: Well, as I showed you in the manual, Art, actuaries show that about two to ten people in your age bracket and in the high-stress type of job you're in are likely to have some sort of disability before they're 45. As you saw on the actuarial report, things like hypertension and heart disease *do* take their toll.

Art: I know all that. But look, I've got a bundle of term insurance with my company.

Harry: But as you know, Art, that insurance is dropped the very minute you leave the company.

Art: I know that.

Harry: Well, wouldn't that put your family in a pretty bad position if something should happen to you?

Art: I suppose.

Harry: According to our profile sheet, Art, I see that you're planning to go into business for yourself. Wouldn't you need the additional coverage even more if you did that?

Art: I suppose. But look, I'm sort of busy now. Talk to me later. I'll think it over.

What caused Art's indifference?

Is Art a prospect for more insurance? On the surface you'd have to say no. He appears to be indifferent to Harry's proposition.

What is the *cause* of Art's indifference? This is the question Harry needs to answer before he can persuade Art to his point of view.

Some of Art's lack of enthusiasm might be chalked up to a natural tendency to resist buying anything. But very likely, his indifference reflects this kind of inner struggle.

Being a responsible — and sensible — family man, Art clearly sees the *logic* of Harry's presentation. On the other hand, he *feels* the need to sustain his country-club lifestyle, rationalizing that it is necessary to his continued business success. Compounding Art's dilemma are a multitude of other marital, business, and social problems whirling around in his head.

How to gain attention

This is the type of confused thinking that Harry must "invade" if he is to get Art's attention. He can gain psychic advantage in this case by breaking through Art's defenses and getting him to voice a concrete objection. Only then will he have a chance to gain psychic advantage and make the sale.

How do you get another person to move from a state of indifference to the point where he will express his *real* feelings? Mainly, by asking the right questions at the right time — and, of course, in the right way. See if Harry does this in the following dialogue:

Harry: Well, Art, do you mind my asking, do you plan to start your own business right away?

Art: What do you mean by right away?

Harry: Well, say within the next year or two?

Art: Oh, yes, within the year.

Harry: Well, don't you think that your insurance needs will be more critical then? Wouldn't your family need more security than ever during this critical period?

Art: I guess so. But look, going into business is tough enough in itself. And it's expensive. Frankly, it's going to take every penny I can get hold of.

Harry: I understand.

Art: That's about it, Harry. I just can't afford it right now.

Harry: That's perfectly all right, Art. As I understand it, your primary concern is being able to afford more insurance at this moment because of your business plans.

Art: That's right.

Harry: Art, if I could somehow give you the coverage you need and at the same time increase your cost only nominally, would you consider my program?

Art: I suppose so. But that doesn't sound realistic.

Harry: But if I *could* show you such a plan, would you go ahead now and give your family the type of security they need?

Art: Well, I guess so.

Harry: Okay, Art, here it is — a program that covers all of your needs. It enables you to pay a relatively low premium now, while you're getting set up in business. Then the premium cost goes up later when you're settled and more able to handle the higher cost.

How to find the real need

Art bought the program. But he wouldn't have bought it if Harry hadn't been able to get him to voice his main objection in the first place. It was only after he learned the real nature of the resistance that he was able to cope with it.

"The *need* was clearly there," Harry said. "But you see, Art had control of *me* so long as he remained indifferent and kept his objections to himself. When I was able to get him to object, *I* gained psychic advantage — at least in my own mind, since I felt certain I could successfully cope with the objection.

How a question gains commitment

"I gained further psychic advantage with what I call a commitment question: 'Would you take the program if I could give you the additional coverage at a nominal increase in cost?' When he agreed, he made a commitment. All I had to do then was to show him how.

"Incidentally, I was selling Art something that filled one of *his* basic needs. This is one of the keys, in my opinion, to being able to win 'arguments.' You can use pressure 'legitimate-ly' when you sell them something that is in their best interest."

Disagree gracefully and let the other person save face

If you're going to persuade others to give up their point of view and accept yours on any given issue, the least you can do is to let the other party save face.

This is as true for nations as it is for individuals. For example, after defeating Germany in W.W. I, the Allies de-manded heavy reparations and largely dismantled German industry. This ultimately created economic chaos, forcing the proud German people into a deep depression. It was under these circumstances that Hitler and his Nazi party took over.

After W.W. II, the Allies were again in the driver's seat. Only this time, they allowed Western Germany to save face. Under the Marshall Plan, they actually helped rebuild the nation they had just defeated. Today, West Germany is a strong and staunch ally. Thus a condition of gaining psychic advan-tage, whether with individuals or with groups, is to enable the other party to face defeat gracefully.

How John Langston dominates the courtroom

John Langston, a successful Texas attorney, has such a strong reputation that he has an immediate psychic advantage over most other lawyers the moment he walks into the court-room. And he rarely disappoints.

In the courtroom he is forceful, eloquent, and almost always totally prepared. On top of this, he is a highly skilled orator, capable of convincing juries with facts or swaying them with an emotional appeal.

Someone as powerful and persuasive as Langston usually creates many enemies, in and out of the courtroom. But Langston is liked, even revered, by most of the attorneys he opposes in the courtroom.

How to disagree gracefully

How does such a strong personality maintain good will — and usually, psychic advantage over others? By doing what almost every successful salesperson has learned to do: He knows how to disagree gracefully and let the other person save face.

Just how do you go about disagreeing gracefully? If you take one position and the other person takes another, doesn't this automatically lead to an argument? Not necessarily. It depends on *how* you disagree; in other words, on whether you *agree before you disagree.*

The principle is so simple that it is indeed surprising that it is used so little in every business and profession, and at every level of negotiation.

Langston vs. Rigby in the courtroom

For example, let's listen in briefly as Langston holds forth in the courtroom. The opposing attorney, J. Arnold Rigby, has just made a very convincing case for his client — so convincing, that you would have to say at this point that he has psychic advantage.

"Ladies and Gentlemen," Langston intones, "Mr. Rigby has just made a very convincing case for his client. He has stated quite accurately, in my opinion, that his client is a highly respected member of our community. He has stated further that his client donates heavily of his time and money to many worthwhile civic projects, which is unquestionably true.

"Mr. Rigby has informed us that his client was *totally*

unaware of the fact that his corporate treasurer, a long and trusted friend, had systematically falsified financial reports over a period of two years and that this resulted in the company's failure to pay over $2 million in corporate taxes. He has suggested, and one can certainly sympathize with his feelings, that a man of Mr. Rigby's stature, wealth, and unassailable character would not knowingly be a party to such a criminal act. Again, I want to congratulate Mr. Rigby for making such an eloquent and convincing case. He is to be congratulated for his attention to detail."

Ending on a dramatic note

Langston paused dramatically at this point, to let his remarks sink in. The feeling among jurors was that he was about to concede the case. Rigby didn't share this feeling; he knew Langston was about to play his trump card. Thus, he waited apprehensively for "the other shoe to drop" — and it did.

At this point, Langston broke the silence with a resounding, "BUT...Ladies and Gentlemen, let us go over the *real* facts, one by one..."

Langston then proceeded to build his case, piece by piece, slowly but surely regaining the psychic advantage that he *seemed* to have lost in throwing bouquets to his opponent.

Langston wins the case and good will

Langston not only won the case, he won the good will and admiration of the opposing attorney and judges alike. Why? Because he has mastered the fine art of disagreeing gracefully and letting the other person save face.

It is extremely difficult to get mad and stay upset with someone who is friendly, smiles at you, and tells you what a wonderful person you are.

We mentioned a moment ago that most successful sales-people are past masters at disagreeing gracefully. Carol Laughton, a high-powered real estate saleslady, is a case in point.

"I didn't do well in real estate at first," she admits. "One of the reasons was that I didn't know how to cope with objections.

A new technique

"Oh, I knew how to parrot the sales manual, all right, but somehow I managed to antagonize people in the process. For example, a prospect would say, 'We'd like to think it over,' and I'd reply, 'Well, the home meets all your requirements. What's there to think over?' Now that I think back, people would seem to tense up when I asked that question. In retrospect, I'd have to say that I probably lost any hope for gaining psychic advantage in the transaction at that point."

Mind you, Carol *was* right. The home did meet the prospect's needs — right size, location, neighborhood, financing, and what have you. The problem was that she was handling the objection in such a way as to rub prospects the wrong way. She seemed to emphasize that she was right and the prospects were wrong.

How the three-F formula works for Carol

"Then I found out from a more experienced salesman about the three-F formula," she said. "It stands for *feel, felt,* and *found.*

"In other words, when someone raises an objection, you say, 'Oh, I know how you *feel.* Others have *felt* the same way. But they *found* that most people liked the neighborhood because once they moved in, they liked the closeness to shopping centers and its high resale value."

The three-F formula is what many veteran salespeople

call a *buffer statement*. The response can be as simple as "I understand" or "I can certainly appreciate your point of view" before trying to handle the objection.

Giving people the "right" to disagree

"You see, when you try to handle an objection head on, so to speak, without a buffer statement, if you're not very careful you'll find yourself in a head-on argument — the very thing you're trying to avoid.

"All you do with the buffer statement is to agree with the prospect's *right* to disagree; not with the position he's taking.

"I would have to say that the buffer statement is the best way I've found to disagree gracefully and to let the other person save face."

It's a super way to avoid an argument and gain psychic advantage.

How to dramatize key points and thoughts

Finding out what another's real problem is and learning to agree before you disagree are key steps in gaining psychic advantage. But the real clincher often lies in being able to get your key point across in an interesting and convincing manner. Advertising people call it *dramatization*. Salespeople call it *showmanship*. By whatever name, it is an excellent way to gain psychic advantage.

For example, Richard White is a salesman for a computer company. One of his biggest problems, he claims, is convincing customers that computers can be used by small companies at a reasonable cost.

"Many of my clients know little about how computers really work, and even less about their cost," White says. "My job is to convince them that they really can't afford to be without one.

Dressing up drab statistics

"So I try to dress up some rather drab statistics like this. I tell them that in 1952 it cost $1.26 to do 100,000 multiplications on a large computer. Six years later — by 1958 — the cost had dropped to 26 cents to perform the same work. By 1964, these same 100,000 multiplications could be done for only 12 cents; and by 1970, for only 5 cents."

White dramatized each point with an illustrated page in his sales manual. He paused for a few minutes before showing the client the last page, which climaxed the "story."

Seeing helps believing

"In the same time frame, Mr. Prospect," he said as he flipped to the last page, "the speed of our computers has been increased from 2,000 multiplications a second to several million multiplications a second. This has decreased the cost of 100,000 multiplications to a fraction of a cent, and the rate will decrease even more as our technology continues to improve."

"It's very important," White added, "that the prospect be able to *see* these figures illustrated in a sales manual or on flip charts of some kind. Otherwise, the figures tend to boggle the imagination and lessen the impact of your story.

"This little demonstration has proved to be very convincing. I'd say that it's what clinches the 'argument' for me in most of my sales."

How Carol gets her "points" across

Carol Laughton, the successful real estate operator mentioned earlier, not only learned to counter objections, she learned to do so with a flair — with drama, that is.

"One of the strongest and most frequent arguments I

get from people trying to sell their homes is that they don't want to pay *discount points,*" Carol says.

Discount points are a "bonus" the seller must pay to the lender if the buyer gets an FHA or VA loan, both of which have lower interest rates than conventional loans. By law, the buyer cannot pay these points.

Selling an "illogical" idea

The idea, though basically a simple one, is hard for most laymen to grasp for a couple of reasons. First, it appears illogical that the seller must pay the sales commission, closing costs, *and* discount points, which can come to several hundred, or even thousand, dollars. Little wonder that most sellers view the matter emotionally. Second, the principle entails explanation of how both financial and bureaucratic institutes operate — a tough job for almost anyone.

Because of these circumstances, Carol gives a heavy buffer statement. "Mr. Prospect, I know *exactly* how you feel. I felt the same way several years ago when I sold my home — and points were even higher than they are today. I didn't like it either...HOWEVER..."

How empathy aids her cause

Having empathized heavily with the seller's plight, Carol launches into a simplified — and illustrated — explanation of points, which she has in her sales manual.

Despite her best efforts, most sellers understandably still don't want to pay points if they can avoid them.

"All right," Carol continues, "we can rule out FHA and VA buyers if you like. But if we do so, we create quite a problem in selling your home."

"What's that?" the prospect asks.

Carol turns slowly to the next page in her sales manual. The pages shows photographs of ten prospective buyers.

She then starts removing the photos one by one until there are only four remaining. "There," she says, "That's what we do by eliminating FHA and VA buyers; we cut out six out of ten buyers who normally buy FHA or VA because of lower interest rates."

Most of Carol's "seers" become believers after this bit of showmanship. It is precisely at this point that she begins to regain psychic advantage in the relationship.

Story-telling as a clincher

Richard White and Carol Laughton frequently use visual aids to dramatize their key points. In addition, they use one of the oldest and most effective argument-winners of all, story-telling.

"Yes, that's true," says Don Carson, a lecturer and management consultant. "My experience has been that most people aren't overly impressed with just a straight factual presentation, however well it's done. They'd rather have lots of 'for instances' — stories, if you will — to get their point across.

"For example, I once had the unenviable job of talking to a group of graduate-level college students on the topic of political systems. The audience was comprised of brilliant young intellectuals who, for the most point, were spoiling for an argument.

Dramatizing a political point

"In preparing my talk, I tried to draw a parallel between our modern political situation in this country and that of other governments that had eventually gone socialistic. Nothing worked. The script seemed flat, academic, and contrived — in short, unconvincing. There was no way this talk would persuade *that* audience. No way I could win an argument here. Finally I got help from a professor friend of mine, who gave me an interesting quote. 'Read it to them in the lecture,' he said, 'and then ask who made this statement and when. I guarantee it'll challenge them and put *you* in the driver's seat.' The quote was: 'The streets of our country are in turmoil. The universities are filled with students rebelling and rioting. Communists are seeking to destroy our country. We are in danger from within and without. What we need now is restoration of law and order. Elect us and I promise you that bringing back law and order to our streets and courts, and our schools, will be our first obligation.'

"The professor was right. Back came the answers: Churchill, Richard Nixon, a young political activist, and so on. All wrong! I played this one to the hilt before finally announcing that the statement was made by Adolph Hitler in a speech in Hamburg, Germany in 1932.

"It definitely got their attention, as did the rest of my talk, which I laced with stories that got my points across."

Most sales organizations realize the value of telling stories to make points and fill their training brochures with them. More often than not, they suggest that salespeople memorize these stories word-for-word.

Stories need warmth, conviction

"There's one thing that you must be very careful of in doing this," said Milt Huffman, regional training director for a national franchise organization. "To be believable, and thus to be effective, a story must have warmth and conviction — a degree of spontaneity. It must *appear* that the salesperson is telling it as it happened if it is to carry real conviction.

"We sometimes warn our salespeople against memorizing a story word-for-word, since it can easily sound 'canned' and actually turn the buyer off. Properly done, a story can clinch your 'argument.' Poorly done, it can have just the opposite effect."

There are few more effective ways of gaining psychic advantage than by using interesting stories to make your point.

How to minimize irrational behavior

Up to this point, we have gained psychic advantage over those who disagree, or object, by analyzing the opposition, disagreeing gracefully, and dramatizing key points.

But what if the other person does not go along with you? What if he is not only irrational, but even a bit hostile in his response? Under these very difficult circumstances, how do you gain the upper hand?

Find out why he's off base

The answer is: by finding the real cause of his unreasonable behavior. In these circumstances, the irrational person cannot normally be convinced by either logic or an emotional appeal. In fact, he probably cannot be convinced at all unless you make an honest attempt to find out *why* he is acting as he is. In most cases, there is a reason, but it does take a skilled practitioner of psychic advantage to ferret it out.

For example, James Blackwell and Cy Atkins are partners in a lucrative real estate business. James has recently taken over the considerable advertising budget and mapped out an extensive TV campaign. He is trying, unsuccessfully up to now, to sell Cy on the program. The conversation goes like this:

James: Look, Cy, we've got a heck of a new TV advertising campaign lined up for next year. I can't understand why you want to stick with the newspapers.

Cy: I've got nothing against the TV spots. We can

still spend a few bucks there. But newspaper is the only way to go.

James: Well, I guess you realize we've got this year's campaign all mapped out. If we go real big with the TV program, we'll get a lot more for our advertising dollar.

Cy: I see where you're coming from, Jim. But I think newspaper's the only way to go, and that's that.

James: Look, Cy, here are the results of the latest Independent Research Advertising League report. They've got no ax to grind, you know, and here's what they say. They say that on television, at least 35 percent of the audience will see our ad on a typical program. And as you can see, that's a much greater audience than you get from newspaper advertising.

Cy: What is it they say about figures: liars, damned liars, and statisticians?

James: It's a reputable outfit. Besides, Cy, you know what kind of reaction we've gotten on our TV ads; it's been tremendous. Why, remember when your little girl first saw you. She was so proud she nearly burst. And remember all those calls you got at the office the next day — just because you appeared in that TV ad.

Cy: Okay, but calls from who? Friends, mostly. Look, we're looking for customers. We're not running a popularity contest.

James: Don't get me wrong, Cy. I can certainly see your point of view. The newspaper *is* an excellent medium. We both know that. It has done us a real job. There's no doubt you've got a strong argument there.

Cy: So let's stick with it, huh?

James: That certainly is a possibility. By the way, Cy, do you mind telling me why it is you're so dead set on using the newspaper format?

Cy: Well, as I say, that's the thing that helped us get where we are today.

James: But you'll also concede the business has changed dramatically since we started, what with the nationwide franchises and all that. Won't you?

Cy: No doubt about that.

James: Well, Cy, tell me, why is it most of the major franchises are switching to TV?

Cy: I haven't given it much thought.

James: Well, I *have*, and I can tell you it's because it's getting results. They're selling a name from coast to coast. In other words, it's institutional advertising, and that's what we need to do if we're to compete.

Cy: Could be, but so what. I'll stick with the newspapers.

James: Market surveys show that TV advertising gets a lot of captive viewers. In other words, the audience more or less *has* to watch the ad. With the newspaper, it's different. The survey shows that the typical newspaper reader won't even turn to the real estate section unless he is specifically looking for a house. That cuts out most of the readers, doesn't it?

Cy: Could be.

James: Cy, do you mind my asking, what is the *real* reason you don't want to advertise on TV?

Cy: Well...there *is* one thing that's bothering me quite a bit, Jim. You know, we've been doing volume business with *The Tribune* for years. They sort of depend on us, and I feel we'll be letting them down if we switch over to TV. You know, there is still such a thing as loyalty.

Reason for attitude

At this point, James has accomplished his mission. He has discovered the real source of Cy's irrational attitude toward television advertising. Now that he knows where to "attack" and with what strategy, he's most likely to persuade Cy to his point of view. He is in a position to gain psychic advantage.

"There is no doubt in my mind that this is the proper way to handle customers who act unreasonable or irrational," says Bill Boland, a veteran sales manager who has seen more than his share of zany customers during over three decades of selling. "There is simply no point in trying to win any kind of argument with this type of person until you have found out what his problem is.

Salespeople often make mistakes

"I know one of the biggest mistakes our young sales-people make is trying to persuade this type of person to their point of view with a strong presentation.

"I tell them to stop trying to sell benefits at this point and to try to find out *why* the other person is acting as he is. If the question is asked properly, they usually don't mind answering. Once you discover the cause of their irrational action, you can start to persuade them to your point of view. Then — and only then — you can gain psychic advantage."

KEY IDEAS

You rarely "win" an argument, since most people, even when confronted with irrefutable logic, still *feel* they at least held their own.

Thus, true persuasion usually involves:

1. Getting the other person to abandon his point of view.
2. Getting him then to accept your point of view.
3. Allowing him to "save face."

Basic steps for increasing your ability to gain psychic advantage in discussion include:

- *Interpreting opposition as interest*
  - Give an emotional reason.
  - Don't accept no as an answer.
  - Recognize resistance as a void.
  - Ask the right questions.
- *Disagreeing gracefully and letting the other person save face.*
- *Dramatizing key points and thoughts*
  - Dress up dead points.
  - Tell a story as a clincher.
- *Minimizing irrational behavior*
  - Determine why he's "off base."

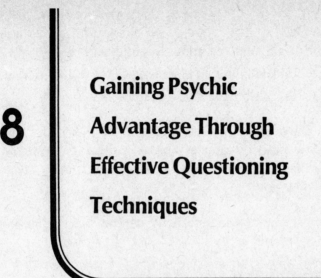

8 Gaining Psychic Advantage Through Effective Questioning Techniques

Someone has suggested that a good question is like a crowbar. It can be used to pry inside another's mind. And this is precisely what psychic advantage is all about, getting into another person's mind.

"Ask a stupid question, get a stupid answer!" Remember that old saw? Well, it's still true. But if you get in the habit of asking meaningful, well-conceived questions, you'll find your control over people and situations will increase enormously.

The benefits of a skillfully posed question

For example, a skillfully posed question can, among other things, enable you to:

- Control a conversation
- Lead another to a desired conclusion
- Challenge a position
- Create a desire

- Manipulate another's thinking pattern
- Uncover a hidden meaning or feeling
- Establish a dominant position

The net result is that you gain control of the conversation and eventually gain psychic advantage over others. Specifically, in this chapter, we'll discuss how to gain this advantage by learning:

- How to use questions as the basis of a *planned* interview
- How to structure questions for best results
- How to make questions "easy" to answer
- How to *lead* others down the path to *your* way of thinking

How to use questions as the basis of a planned presentation

Know the answer you want, and it's easy enough to come up with the right question. This principle is used at times by virtually every professional "interviewer," and it is one of the most effective techniques known for controlling people and situations.

For example, let's assume that I hand you a deck of cards and ask you to select a card *without your looking at it*. I now know that the card is the six of clubs, but *you do not know what the card is*. I now know what questions to ask to get the "right" answer. This is the way my query would go:

"There are four suits," I say. "Two are red and two are black. Which do you select?"

"Red."

"Okay, and if it isn't red, it will be?"

"Black."

"Fine. Now of the black suits, which do you select — spades or clubs?"

"Clubs."

"Good. Now in the club suit there are thirteen cards. The numbered cards, one through ten, and the face cards. Which do you select?"

"Face cards."

"And if it isn't a face card, it's what?"

"Numbered."

"Right. And of the numbered cards, you have one through five in the lower bracket and six through ten in the upper. Which do you select?"

"Upper."

"Right. And in this group, we have six and seven in the lower bracket and nine and ten in the upper. Which do you choose?"

"Lower."

"And of the six and seven, which do you choose?"

"The seven."

"And if it isn't the seven, it's what?"

"The six of clubs."

"Right on the money."

How a salesman uses the "yes-conditioning" technique

It was this very principle that converted Jim Blackburn from a mediocre to a highly successful real estate salesman. In sales work in general, this technique is called "yes-conditioning" a customer. In other words, if the buyer responds affirmatively to a series of your preconceived, or planned questions, he obviously ends up agreeing with *your* position. The technique was first used in the dialogues of Plato and Aristotle, and it is often called the Platonic method of questioning.

A glib talker, Jim at first relied on his "gift of gab" to talk homeowners into listing their property with him. "I was doing all right," he said, "but I wasn't *consistently* getting my fair share of listings."

A thorough analysis of his interviews revealed Jim's problem. He felt that he was at the mercy of sellers. If he didn't list the home, he didn't have "merchandise" to sell. Thus, he let sellers ask most of the questions and, in effect, control the interview.

Using a planned presentation

"It was at this point that I began to think of a sales presentation as an 'interview,'" Jim said, "and of myself as the interviewer. 'What makes for a good interviewer?' I asked myself. And suddenly it occurred to me: It is the ability to control the conversation through effective questions."

Jim promptly wrote down the information he needed from the typical homeowner. He then formed — and memorized — key questions that would net him that information. From this analysis came this planned question format:

- Have you had any offers on your home?
- How long have you had your home on the market?
- What price are you asking and what is the basis of that price? May we offer you a market analysis to help you arrive at a fair price?
- Have you been advertising in the newspaper?
- Why are you selling?
- Have you arranged for financial and legal assistance? If not, may I assist you in these important areas, without obligation?

"I now have the questions completely memorized, and I ask them in this sequence on every interview, if I possibly can," Jim said. "The results have been fantastic. My listings have almost doubled. My confidence in my ability to get listing appointments has soared. This is mainly because I now know that through these questions I can control the interview and in most cases get an appointment. That's what a planned presentation based on solid questions has done for me."

Jim found that if a planned interview format worked in one area of selling it would work in another. He drew up a series of questions to use in qualifying buyers and another to use in answering phone calls on ads. His efficiency increased dramatically in these areas, too.

Almost any salesperson can, like Jim, increase his or her ability to *control* clients a great deal by basing the interview on a carefully thought out series of questions. The principle is equally effective in any type of interview, providing the skilled interviewer a distinct psychic advantage.

Controlling the interview

Specific questions can't always be worked out beforehand. However, a general line of questioning can often net the same results — control of the interview and psychic advantage in the relationship.

For example, Jim found that he was losing many buyers who wanted to "think it over." The objection is often genuine, but more often than not it reflects a "hidden objection," something the buyer doesn't want to discuss with the salesperson. This obviously gives the client a clear psychic advantage in the negotiation, since the salesperson doesn't even know what the problem is, or *if* there is one.

Regaining control

How did Jim learn to uncover the real problem? How did he regain psychic advantage? Through a planned questioning technique. For example:

"When the buyer says 'I want to think it over,' I immediately agree that it is indeed a big decision and warrants considerable thought," Jim said. "However, I tell the prospective buyers I'd like to help them. And then, without really waiting for permission, I start firing a series of questions at them.

"'Is it the location?' I ask.

"'No, the location is fine.'

"'How about the price? Is that bothering you?'

"'It's a little steep, but I think we can swing it.'

"'The down payment?'

"'No. No problem there.'

"'How about the schools? Are they close enough for you?'

"'They could be closer. But that's no real problem.'

"'Well, Mr. Prospect, how about the monthly payment? You seemed to be a little concerned when we were figuring it out.'

"'Well, to tell the truth...yes, it is more than we had planned to pay.'

"As of this moment," Jim continued, "I have regained control of the interview. I now know what the *real* problem is and have some chance of helping the buyer to resolve his problem and hopefully to make his decision then and there."

Had the buyer not objected to anything, Jim would have gained a concession that there was no objection and perhaps no real reason for not buying. Or he would at least have found out that the objection was a genuinely conservative reaction.

Jim was reasonably sure that the answer in each instance would be no (which really meant yes), since he had put them in the right location, the right price bracket, and so forth. Here again, he knew the right question because he knew the answer. The best way to control an interview with another, whether you're a Johnny Carson interviewing in a national talk show, or a personnel director hiring professional people, is to plan your interview in advance. It's perhaps the most effective way of making sure that you control the interview.

How to structure questions for best psychic results

Different types of questions are designed to net different answers. For example, when a personnel director asks a prospective employee, "Do you enjoy detail work?" the question begs a yes or no answer. This is a *direct* question, and its main function is to elicit a specific and normally limited answer. It was a series of direct questions, you'll recall, that enabled Jim to find out specifically *what* the I-want-to-think-it-over buyer had in mind.

On the other hand, the personnel director might ask a prospective employee an *indirect*, or open-end question, such as, "What did you like — or dislike — about detail work?" The applicant is virtually compelled to give an *opinion*. And this is the prime purpose of the indirect question — to draw people out.

How to use reflective questions

There is still a third type of question that you can use to gain psychic advantage. It is the *feedback*, or reflective, question, which goes like this: "Mr. Jones, as I understand it, you left your last job because you felt the pay was inadequate and you weren't able to use your full talents. Is this correct?" The purpose here is to clarify or pin down another's point of view — a point on which he might or might not have been clear himself. This type of question is frequently helpful, since many do not clearly state what is on their mind.

All three types of questions — direct, indirect, and feedback — can be used at various times to help you gain psychic advantage over others.

For instance, a personnel director would appear to have a clear psychic advantage in interviewing a job applicant, and in most cases does. But the applicant is not without "advantages" in that he can omit, slant, or distort information. After all, all details about an applicant can't be traced. The applicant can sometimes hide things that he doesn't want the interviewer to know — say a drinking or "personality" problem. However, a highly skilled interviewer can neutralize this "advantage" by drawing out such information with an indirect questioning technique.

The uses of indirect interviewing

For example, Walt Stockton is personnel director for a Fortune 500 company that recruits many management people from outside the company. "For awhile," he said, "my track record for hiring executives was pretty lousy. Then I began to use a technique some call *indirect interviewing.* The method is based on listening more and, in a sense, asking less. Such an interview might go like this:

"Overall, you certainly have excellent credentials, Mr. Jones," Walt would say. "But right here, I notice you say you left your last job because of a personality clash..." Walt pauses and looks direct at Jones.

Jones finally breaks what to him seems an interminable silence. "Why, yes, I felt there was no way I could continue working for him. He was just too dictatorial."

"Dictatorial?"

"Yes, I guess that's the right word. He'd never take my word for anything. Always checking up. Look, I'm a professional person, and I just can't do my job with someone looking over my shoulder."

"Looking over your shoulder?"

"Well, what I mean is, he would check up to see if I

got to work on time. Check to see how long I took for lunch. Check to see if I left before 5 o'clock."

"For no reason?"

"That's right. Well, it probably all started with a little problem we had when I went to work there five years ago."

"Little problem?"

"Well, yes. I had just gotten a divorce at the time, and I guess you might say for a short period I had a little drinking problem. I guess I missed a few days here and there."

"Oh?"

"But that's all in the past. In fact, I haven't missed a day's work in the past year."

The conversation continued in this vein, with Jones revealing the background and nature of a rather erratic work history.

Notice the frequency — and especially the brevity — of the questions: "Dictatorial?" "Looking over your shoulder?" "For no reason?" "Oh?" The questions in each instance were just enough to keep Jones talking, and in this case, enough to reveal the real nature of his problem. So though Jones was "dominating" the conversation, it was Walt who was using a subtle questioning technique to draw out facts that otherwise would not have surfaced.

How to ask the "unanswerable"

Walt's ability to stage indirect interviews has been especially valuable to him — and his company — in view of existing policies against discrimination.

For example, it is generally unlawful these days to ask an applicant any question that might be used to discriminate against him or her. This obviously would include queries about age, sex, religion, marital status, and so forth. Technically, it is even unlawful to ask an applicant if he has transportation, or in the case of a married woman, whether she has someone who can take care of her children.

Determining marital status

Obviously, Walt frequently needs to get some of this information in order to properly assess the applicant. How does he get it? Through indirect questioning.

Instead of asking about marital status, for example, he might ask an applicant, "Will your having to travel present any particular problems with your family?" "Why, no," the applicant is likely to respond, "both of my children are in school until 3:30 every day. And besides, my husband frequently gets home before I do."

Has Walt avoided the law? Of course not — the applicant "volunteered" the information.

Asking about age

"Age" is a particularly sensitive issue. But again, Walt gets around this one with adroit indirect questioning, as reflected in this excerpt from an interview:

Walt: I notice you're wearing an Air Force Association pin. Which chapter do you belong to?

Applicant: The Dallas group.

Walt: Well, that's interesting. I spent a little time in the Air Force.

Applicant: Yeah? What did you fly?

Walt: F-104s for the most part.

Applicant: Jets, huh? Well, you're a little after my time. I flew the old prop jobs — P-51s to be exact. Remember them?

Indeed Walt did remember, and it placed the applicant

in a World War II time frame. From there, it was relatively easy to arrive at the applicant's approximate age.

Using silence effectively

An integral part of the indirect interviewing technique is *silence*. Notice, that in the case of Jones, Walt remained silent for a relatively long period after his opening question. The silence gave Walt psychic advantage for a couple of reasons. First, the silence for all practical purposes "told" Jones, "I'm listening to what you have to say, but you haven't said enough. Tell me more." Second, the strategy was effective in determining how Jones would react in a pressure situation. Had Jones shown signs of being intimidated or attempted to avoid the subject, Walt would have probed further in this area.

In either case, strategic use of silence is a way of putting legitimate pressure on another and gaining psychic advantage. The technique is used quite frequently by veteran salespeople as a way of gaining a degree of psychic advantage over a client. "When I ask a closing question, I remain absolutely silent," a veteran clothing salesman said. "The first one who speaks 'loses.'"

"The more questions you ask, the more you'll keep the applicant talking," Walt said. "The more he talks and the more you listen, the greater advantage you'll gain."

"For example, I used to make the mistake of telling an applicant everything there was to know about our company — plus some interesting sidelights he wouldn't have normally known for months. I was just trying to be helpful. Then it dawned on me that I was giving the applicant 'ammunition' with which to answer questions I'd ask later in the interview. In other words, this information enabled him to *slant* his answers to give me the answer I wanted to hear. I've changed all that now, and I start the interview with open-end questions.

This way, I'm more likely to get his *real* feelings about the company. This has helped reduce our executive turnover rate."

Naturally, Walt has a host of routine *planned* questions for job applicants. Questions like: What prompted you to leave your last job? What do you know about our company? What are your future plans? And so forth.

But it is the more sophisticated questioning techniques — such as the Platonic method of direct questioning and the indirect method of interviewing — which enable Walt to consistently maintain psychic advantage.

How to make questions "easy" to answer

The story goes around that a young priest entering the service asked the Bishop, "Is it all right if I smoke while I pray?"

"Definitely not," the Bishop replied, "and frankly, I'm quite disappointed that you would even ask."

Dejected, the young priest later related the incident to an older priest. "Well," the older priest said, "I asked the same question 20 years ago and got a little different answer. I'm afraid you asked the question in the wrong way."

"How's that?" the young priest said.

"Nothing to it," the older priest said. "I simply asked the Bishop, 'Is it all right to pray while I smoke?'

"'Of course,' the Bishop replied, 'and how dedicated of you.'"

People don't like "hard" questions

As a rule, people dislike your asking "hard" questions but like your posing a question they find "easy" to answer. Thus, if you can ask a question that is easy for them to answer and at the same time yields the answer *you* want, you have made a "friend" and gained psychic advantage in the same breath.

A classic example of using such a strategy occurred some years ago with a leading drug store chain. Customers were being asked, "Do you want an egg in your malt?" and they were saying no in droves. But soda jerks were later instructed to pose the question differently. "Good morning, would you like one egg or two in your malt today?" Many who had not previously had an egg in their malt would take one, but rarely two. The point is, they took *something*.

How car salesmen use this technique

The same principle is at work when a car salesman asks, "Would you like to have your free car initials in Old English or just plain letters?" Or when the real estate broker asks a seller, "Will you need 30 days before you can give possession or will you take a little longer, say 45 days?" Or when a booking agent asks, "Would you rather meet in Chicago this year or in Dallas?"

In effect, the car salesman was asking, "Will you buy a car?" The real estate broker was saying, "Will you list your house?" The booking agent was saying, "Will you let us book your meeting?" But all of these are *tough* questions that buyers are reluctant to answer outright; thus, they remain in the driver's seat in the relationship. However, the simplified versions are "easy" to answer, and they are likely to switch the psychic advantage to the salesmen and the booking agent.

A simple way to gain psychic advantage

This principle, which we'll call the easy-question or choice-between-two-positives approach, can be applied in almost any situation where you are trying to gain a commitment from another. It is a deceptively simply way to gain psychic advantage.

I say deceptively simple because such questions are almost always hard to come up with on the spur of the moment. This means, of course, that they must be *planned* beforehand.

Why does such a technique work so well? For several reasons. In the first place, most of us are suggestible; we tend to follow suit, to join the bandwagon. If an associate orders a club sandwich, we order a club sandwich. If the boss wears French cuffs, we wear French cuffs. If someone asks, "Do you want one egg or two in your malt," we tend to answer, "Just one," because we *assume* everyone does it.

The key word is *suggestible.* When you pose a question that suggests a course of action, and when that question is in addition easy to answer, you've likely gained a high degree of psychic advantage in your association.

The power of the "reverse question"

There is still another technique used by Joe Barnes and many other successful salespeople. It is what Joe calls a reverse-question or question-with-question technique. Though they are slightly different in application, the techniques will net you the same result — control, and thus psychic advantage, over the other person.

"It works like this," Joe says, "a client will ask, 'I wonder if the owner will take $70,000 for that boat?' I then simply reverse the question and ask, 'Would you like me to ask if he'll take $70,000?' When the client says yes, why of course he has really made an offer.

"The logic here is simple. When a person asks such a question, it almost always indicates that he's interested in making an offer, but he'd rather not come right out and say so. This would strip him of the psychic advantage he has as a buyer. I make it *easy* for my customers by simply turning their questions back to them when it seems appropriate."

Joe's theory jibes with what psychologists say. If a person flatly asserts he's buying another's product because it's cheaper, he probably is. But if he asks, "Why should I buy your product when I can get it cheaper elsewhere?" he's saying in effect that if you can tell him *why,* he might do business with you. In other words, the question indicates there's a void to be filled; if you can fill it, you "win."

How to answer a question with a question

The question-with-question technique is a tremendously effective way of controlling a conversation, especially one in which the other party has the upper hand psychologically.

For example, this situation occurs routinely with Jim Blackburn, the real estate salesman, when prospective buyers answer ads placed by Jim's company in the newspaper. "Callers are usually defensive," Jim says. "They don't want to get involved with a salesperson, so they simply try to get all the information they can while giving as little as possible. In other words, they want to control the conversation, and they have the advantage of not only withholding information but of hanging up."

Here is the way Jim typically handles such calls in order to capture psychic advantage:

"I'm calling about the 'Colonial Home' you have advertised. Can you give me the price please?"

"Yes, the price is $60,000. Is that the range you had in mind?"

"Possibly, but we'd have to see it. Where is it located?"

"It's on Walton Avenue on the South Side. Is this the area you had in mind?"

"I think so. Incidentally, I see the existing loan is assumable. Can you tell me what the equity is?"

"Yes, I can. It's $33,000. Is this the amount you wished to invest?"

"No, that's too much. We just couldn't swing that at all. Not over $15,000 down at the outside."

"Well, we could arrange for other financing, or perhaps we could show you some others in the area where $15,000 would get you in a comparable home. Would you care to drive by the office or can I pick you up at your place of business?"

"We'll just meet you in the office in about 30 minutes if you'll give us the location."

"Fine. It's at 2832 Walraven Circle."

Who controlled the interview? Jim Blackburn, of course. How? Essentially by answering a question with a question. Otherwise, the caller would have simply gotten the information requested — including the address — and never shown up on Jim's prospect list.

Though the caller unquestionably had psychic advantage going into the conversation, Jim wrested it from him by a simple but effective questioning technique — answering a question with a question. It works.

How to lead others to your way of thinking

Remember the lawyer who asked the frustrated witness, "Are you still beating your wife?" The lawyer's strategy, of course, is to lead the witness to a hasty or ill-conceived response; in effect, to psyche him out.

The legal profession is one in which psychic advantage is truly imperative. Lawyers renowned for their oratorical prowess in the courtroom probably win many cases on reputation alone. Judicial restraints undoubtedly preclude such blatantly slanted questions as, "Are you still beating your wife?" But psychically strong barristers like Hamilton B. of Oklahoma can literally dominate a courtroom with their skillful questioning techniques.

How do you develop this expertise? "Mainly by developing psychologically sound techniques and practicing them routinely," Hamilton said. "I always try to remember that the advantage rests with the witness so long as he can withhold information that I need. About the only way I can get the information out of him is through skillful questioning."

The either-or strategy

For example, Hamilton is a past master, as are many members of the legal fraternity, at using the *either-or* concept, a strategy frequently used by propagandists.

"As an example," Hamilton said, "I might ask a witness, 'Do you favor or oppose the compensation program?' Given two choices representing opposite views, many witnesses are inclined to take one or the other, oblivious to the fact that they might be neutral on the subject. Thus, the person is *led* to give an answer — and impression — that he might not have given had the question been phrased differently.

"I've also learned," Hamilton continued, "that people are more likely to give a favorable response when asked if they are *for* rather than against something. In other words, questions phrased positively rather than negatively stand a better chance of acceptance. This is another way of leading an individual to the answer *you* want."

For instance, a question like, "Should the city government go into debt to support the new program?" is likely to draw a preponderantly negative response. It suggests a no answer through language and tone. Rephrased in a positive vein, such as, "Should the city government issue new bonds to support the progressive new program?" the question is more likely to receive a favorable response.

Naturally, it takes much practice to reach the point where you can phrase such questions more or less on the spot. But this is precisely the point. In order to gain psychic advantage routinely, it is first necessary to recognize and adopt these

strategies and then to practice them until they become second
nature.

The use of conditioning phrases

Another way to gain psychic advantage through questioning is to lead another by "conditioning" him with highly
suggestible introductory phrases such as, "As you know..."
"According to law (or some other generally accepted source)..."
"The way things stand now..." "As we both know..." "Isn't
it true that..." Such phrases strongly suggest the status quo.
For instance, a salesperson might say, "The way the market has
been lately, your property is almost certain to sell quickly, don't
you think?" The question begs agreement.

Another way of gaining what might be called limited
psychic advantage is to use all-inclusive terms, such as *never,
always, all, none, everybody,* and the like. For example, how
would you, as an unsuspecting adversary, tend to answer the
following questions: "Does your boss *always* show up at work
before the office staff?" "Do *any* of your people like the new
retirement plan?" "Is it *ever* wise to drop by a client's office
without calling first?"

My experience is that when people answer such questions they "listen" right past such terms as *always, any,* and
ever and answer as if these words were not used at all in the
question. Their answer to these questions would more often
than not be yes, which would, of course, be generally incor-
rect. The boss is usually there before anyone else, but not always. While most like the new retirement plan, a handful don't.
And while 99.9 percent of the time it's wise to call a client first,
there are rare exceptions where this is not true.

So, depending on the nature of your question, you can
confuse an issue — and an adversary — by timely usage of
vague questions with all-inclusive terms.

The point is, few listeners are perceptive enough to
analyze the semantic overtones of a question. When respond-

ing to a question such as, "Do authorities have a moral obligation to prevent widespread distribution of pornographic
literature?" they tend to respond without a proper frame of
reference for such terms as *moral obligation, widespread distribution,* and *pornographic literature.* Obviously such terms
must be defined before you can give a meaningful answer.

How to use the direct challenge

Skilled questioners such as many lawyers, reporters,
and salespeople use a number of other questions to gain control
of the conversation and ultimately to gain psychic advantage.

One way is to literally *challenge,* a technique that can
be used to play on another's pride. "We have found, Mr. Prospect," the salesperson says, "that our system works quite well
for a conglomerate, but this might pose some real problems for
an independent operator like yourself." "What do you mean?"
the small business owner responds indignantly. "Look, we can
do anything the big boys can do. Maybe more."

A similar technique is employed by an encyclopedia
company when a customer gains the "upper hand" with the
enigmatic objection, "We want to think it over. Why don't you
give us a call tomorrow." Psychic advantage at this point lies
clearly with the customer. "Sorry," the salesman responds, "but
our finding is that if people don't buy our product the first time
around, either they don't thoroughly understand the proposition we're asking them to buy, or quite frankly, they simply
cannot afford it." It's a calculated risk, but the strategy often
puts the advantage back with the salesman, since many buy as
a result of this lightly intimidating strategy.

Getting a commitment through clarification

I have personally found that another effective way to
gain control of the conversation is to frequently *clarify* another's
remarks. "Mr. Smith, as I understand it, you're convinced we

need a new facility, but you're unwilling to float a bond program to finance it. Is that correct?"

The technique can readily net you psychic advantage for a couple of reasons. First, people rarely say precisely what they have in mind, and this is one good way to "prove" it. Second, it gives *you* a chance to state *his* position in *your* terms, enabling you to embellish or slant his remarks as you see fit. And if you happen to be both crafty and articulate, you can likely slant the meaning more in your favor.

Still another method is to ask a favor of another. "Mr. Prospect, would you be willing to help me solve a problem I've had for some time now?" This is an implied compliment, and assuming it doesn't cost the other person time or money, he's usually willing to go along with the idea. Again, you have gained a degree of psychic advantage.

In summary, take pains to:

- Plan your questions ahead of time.
- Make your questions as easy to answer as possible.
- Structure your questions so that the answer comes out in your favor.
- Learn methods for leading the other person to your way of thinking.

Having done these things, you've taken a giant stride toward gaining psychic advantage over others.

KEY IDEAS

A skillfully phrased question is like a crowbar; it can help you "pry" into another's mind and, ultimately, to gain psychic advantage.

Specific questioning techniques you'll need to master include:

- *Using questions as the basis of a planned interview*
  - Keep control of the interview.
  - "Yes condition" with the Platonic technique.
- *Structuring questions for best psychic results*
  - Use the direct question.
  - Exploit fully the indirect question.
  - Master the reflective question.
  - Employ "silence" for effect.
- *Making questions easy to answer*
  - Give a choice between two positives.
  - Use reverse questions.
  - Answer a question with a question.
- *Leading others down the path to your way of thinking*
  - Develop and practice various techniques.
  - Perfect the either-or method.
  - State your question in a positive vein.
  - Use leading phrases.
  - Adopt the "challenge" technique.

9

How to Achieve
Psychic Advantage
by Reading Body
Types and Language

Your body is one of your best bets for gaining psychic advantage. It depends on how it's "built" and how well it "speaks."

We're talking about "body language," the facial and body movements and gestures through which you communicate continuously. What's more, there's a fast-growing group of experts who think they can predict behavior by observing your body build — whether you're fat, skinny, short, tall, or in between.

The goal here is to master body language and body watching so that you can control people and situations more expertly.

Developing a defensive strategy

There's also the other side of the coin. Thanks to a rash of publications on the subject, people now generally know a good deal about the fine art of body language. So much so, in fact, that you'll very likely have to develop a defensive strategy to compensate for this fact.

For example, most people now recognize that a raised eyebrow is a sign of disbelief. Knowing this, you can use this sign at the "right" time to get your message across. Or, you can use it at the "wrong" time to throw your adversary off guard. This same idea holds true for all the universally accepted body signs.

The point is this: If you're "winning" most of your body-language "encounters," you can become even more effective; if you're "losing," you can learn to make up for your deficiencies by developing superior defensive strategems.

The benefits to be gained

Once you've mastered this "body knowledge," you'll be able to more successfully:

- Uncover and exploit hidden meanings
- Cope with those who possess superior skills
- Turn the tables on would-be manipulators
- Predict and neutralize tactics of others
- Outmaneuver would-be opportunists

The specific areas you'll need to master include:

- Coding and decoding others' messages
- Masking your emotions; unmasking others'
- Successfully invading the other's territory
- How to read and use body types

Coding and decoding others' messages

By now you're probably familiar — consciously or sub-consciously — with the meaning of the most *basic* facial and body movements and gestures.

If another person slaps his forehead in apparent dismay, he's probably forgotten something. If he raises his eyebrows at something you say or do, he's either surprised or doesn't believe you. If he rubs his nose as you try to explain something, he's likely a bit confused, or perhaps puzzled is a better word for it. If he purses his lips and wrinkles his brow, he's very likely thinking seriously about what you're saying.

On the other hand, if he taps his fingers impatiently, sighs, yawns, or happens to look away repeatedly as you talk, let's face it, he's bored, or at best indifferent to your proposition. If he goes a step further and crosses his arms, he's not only bored, he's openly resisting you. A woman who assumes the same posture, and in addition crosses her legs, is offering maximum resistance to any idea — or advance — you might have in mind.

What the eyes reveal

Then there are the eyes, undoubtedly the most expressive part of the human makeup. Someone once put it this way; "Your face might lie, but your eyes can't."

Eyes can reveal the gamut of emotions. Half-closed eyes usually reflect a sensuous state. Wide-open eyes express amazement or delight. Closed eyes reveal exasperation, or possibly even a desire to sleep.

Actually, it is the pupil, the dark spot in the middle of the eye, that unconsciously gives you away. When you're excited, the pupil expands rather rapidly. This is an important point to remember when you feel someone is trying to hide their true feelings.

But as revealing as the eyes are, it is what we *do* with them that often tells an even more complete story about the human scene.

Stares for the non-person

For example, a wink usually says, "I like you," "You're cute," "I understand your situation completely," or "We know, don't we?" Or, it can be simply a sign of egotism on the winker's part.

Then there's the *stare*, a deadly weapon in the battle for psychic advantage. Society says it's impolite in public to hold a glance for over a few seconds. When you do so, you're in effect telling the other person, "I can look at you all I want, since I'm superior." Stares are usually reserved for non-persons: derelicts and others of low station.

Why constant surveillance is needed

There are other body gestures and movements, and there are many variations of those just mentioned. But these are the basic ones from which you can plan your master strategy for gaining psychic advantage by coding and decoding others' nonverbal messages.

The idea here is simply this. The more you study and analyze people and their movements, the more you will come to discover that people tell us many things without saying a word. And though most of these signs are universal in meaning, each of us has gestures and movements which, when used in a certain context, "say" certain things. To gain psychic advantage over others, you must become even more adept at picking up these signals.

Looking for "messages"

Learning to interpret and use nonverbal messages can be an invaluable asset in your business and social affairs. Sometimes, these nonverbal cues communicate more clearly than words themselves.

For example, the president of a U.S. conglomerate has a reputation for being a sort of Jekyll-and-Hyde character. One moment he's considerate and rather easy-going, the next he's unpredictable and overbearing, badgering and intimidating even his closest lieutenants.

Part real, part acting

Part of the president's changeable personality is real; to a degree, he *is* moody. However, an even larger part of it is contrived, and for good reason — it keeps people off guard, enabling him to sustain a relatively high degree of psychic advantage over most people. But to a lesser degree over his secretary, who can "read him like a book."

"The secret," she says, "is to know *when* he's going to be 'Jekyll' and *when* he wants to play 'Hyde.' Then you simply adjust *your* mood and actions to his."

Know-how is the key

The key, of course, is to know *when* the president is about to assume which personality. And how did the secretary discover this secret? By "reading" his gestures and mannerisms.

"It occurred to me one day that just before he went into one of his bad moods he started stroking the back of his head. Don't ask me why, but it was at that precise moment that I tied the stroking of his head and the bad mood together. I naturally checked out my new-found theory, and sure enough it was valid. They went together like ham and eggs. So now, every time he starts stroking the back of his head, I start getting ready for one of his tirades."

Finding "clues"

The secretary attached no deep-seated significance to this gesture as a body language expert would tend to do. Still, advanced students of psychic advantage normally detect the significance of such gestures and movements because they are looking for them.

After successfully finding a clue to the "bad mood," the secretary theorized that there must be another clue for the boss's better moods. Sure enough, she was right. The president tipped off his happier moods by walking around with his hands on his hips — almost strutting, you might say. The connection? Again, there is none, really. It's peculiar to him, and it really doesn't matter.

How Bill Lawrence closes deals

For example, Bill Lawrence, a successful Oklahoma City real estate broker, has developed into a top-notch closer, thanks in part to his ability to read "body messages" sent by his clients.

"It took me some time to recognize this particular signal," Bill said, "but after a while, I began to notice that some clients would cross their legs and lean forward when they were about ready to sign a contract. By this movement, the client was telling me in so many 'words' that he was ready to close the transaction. It doesn't *always* work this way, of course. But I'll tell you one thing. When my client assumes this posture, I *try* a close. And nine times out of ten, it'll work."

How Peggy Jackson reads clients

Peggy Jackson of Fort Worth, who also sells millions of dollars in property annually, is likewise a strong believer that action speaks louder than words. She is constantly on the lookout for that "knowing glance" between husband and wife that says go or no go when it comes to buying the house.

"I can't exactly explain it," Peggy admits, "but it's a certain look between the two. The wife's look says, 'What do you think?' and the husband's glance says, 'Looks great to me,' without a word being spoken." Of course, the glance often reveals a resounding no, in which case, Peggy immediately starts to show other properties.

The better you get to know people, the greater your chances of being able to pick up their individual body language style.

For example, Mel Turner, an erstwhile advertising account executive, had great difficulty selling his ideas to a particularly tough manufacturer until he learned to read the owner's movements correctly.

How an ad man gained psychic advantage

"This guy was really inscrutable," Turner said. "He was probably a great poker player; no tipoff at all as to how he felt about our campaign proposal. I noticed that about the only thing he did with any consistency was to occasionally clasp his hands behind his head and frown. Naturally, I felt this to be a sign of superiority, and of course, rejection of my idea.

"Then it dawned on me one day that this was precisely the posture he would assume before accepting a campaign. In other words, the superior attitude and frown were really defensive gestures. He was upset because he wasn't sure he should be spending money on this kind of campaign anyway.

"So nowadays when he assumes this familiar position, I take the offensive and start reeling off the benefits. He's looking for assurance that he's spending his money wisely, and this is exactly what I give him. It's not long before I have complete control of the situation."

Clients constantly seek assurance

Many salespeople have found that quite a few customers get nervous and irascible just before they say yes. The reason is that they're going through the throes of making a decision. They want assurance that they're making the *right* decision.

The salesperson who can detect this and give this assurance can gain a high degree of control in the relationship.

When corrective action is needed

Reading the other person's body talk must, of course, be followed by appropriate "corrective" action.

For example, a salesperson tells a client that his firm can offer its services for at least 20 percent less than competitors. Whereupon, the client raises not one but both eyebrows.

The message: "I don't believe a word you're saying." The remedy: "Mr. Jones, I know this sounds like another sales claim, but let me show you the report put out last month by the National Trade Association for the industry..."

Fidgeting spells unrest

Or, let's assume you're a manager reviewing a comprehensive financial report for the board of directors. As you do, the chairman drums his fingers on the table, fidgets in his chair, and sighs. The message: "Get on with it, man." The remedy: "Gentlemen, here's a quick rundown on the production figures. It's there in detail if you want to read it and ask me questions later." In so doing, you have just regained control.

But this sort of effort is defensive in nature and only gives you limited control. To gain true psychic advantage, you must use your knowledge of body language in an even more productive fashion.

How athletes use this knowledge

In the highly competitive world of sports, athletes who succeed often do so not through talent alone, but by being able to pinpoint and exploit opponents' weaknesses.

Professional football and baseball teams spend hours watching game films and listening to scouting reports on opposing clubs. Professional boxers study their upcoming opponents with perhaps even greater intensity, hoping to find some flaw in style — some movement that will telegraph the punches. If they find such clues, they can sometimes enter the fray with a pronounced psychological edge.

If you will be equally observant in seeking out the other person's telltale body movements and facial gestures, you can gain the same kind of psychic advantage over people and situations.

Masking your emotions; unmasking others'

Using your knowledge of body language to regain control of the situation is laudable. But remember, the ultimate goal is to *gain psychic advantage*. This you can learn to do by first masking your real feelings so that others cannot "see" how you feel and then by sending out *false* signals of your own to purposely confuse the issue.

For example, let's say one woman says to another, "I saw your husband having lunch with his secretary downtown yesterday." The comment is calculated to evoke a hostile response. The "wronged" lady is supposed to raise her eyebrows indignantly and say something like, "Are you sure it was Joe?"

But this is precisely what she is supposed to do. And this is precisely why this startling bit of information was passed along in the first place, to give the gossiper psychic advantage.

Step one: mask feelings

If you get caught in such a situation, the idea is to think and *act* fast. First, mask your feelings of surprise and indignation, simply by looking her in the eye and saying oh and winking knowingly before adding, "How interesting. And how are you and your third husband getting along?"

Who has the psychic advantage now? You do, of course. She is wondering what you know that she doesn't know. It must be something; otherwise, you would have acted more predictably. You have confused her with your enigmatic action. As discussed earlier, one of the hallmarks of power is to develop an aura of mystery. Leave a little, and sometimes a lot, to the other person's imagination.

Sending false alarms

Sending false messages to confuse is a firmly established military strategy. For example, if the Air Force were planning to bomb a vital target in the North, they would send a few bombers to the South to divert the enemy's attention. Or, if they were to get word of an incoming missile or enemy bomber, they would immediately send out electronic decoys to confuse the incoming weapons.

Similarly, when someone tries to gain control of your psyche through devious means, throw up a smokescreen by masking your real feelings and then by "counterattacking" with a gesture or movement that will throw him completely off guard and restore psychic advantage to you.

Rehearsing evasive tactics

The evasive tactics should be well rehearsed. For example, in the foregoing story, the anticipated response would logically have been one of surprise and probably shock. The point is, you generally have to practice *not* showing surprise in order to carry out your counterattack successfully. There are several ways to do this.

Dark glasses hide reactions

One way to keep your eyes from giving you away is to wear dark glasses to any meeting in which you *suspect* that someone might be trying to pick your psyche. The glasses can be fairly light; in fact, not much more than tinted glasses. They simply have to "hide" the pupil, the tiny "dot" in the middle of the eye that expands when you're excited, thus revealing your true emotions. The pupil and the movement of the area around the eyes give away true feelings.

If you question the soundness of such a tactic, or the fact that it can be used to give you psychic advantage, consider the case of the late Aristotle Onassis, one of the world's wealthiest men. Being essentially an emotional, demonstrative man, the Greek shipping magnate realized that his eyes might betray him in one of his high-powered financial transactions. As a result, he would frequently wear dark glasses — in fact, they became sort of a trade mark — to important business deals. The strategy seems to have worked quite well.

Naturally, it's not always practical to have dark glasses around or to wear them. Hence the necessity of developing some evasive eye tactics of your very own.

Other diversionary eye tactics

For example, the minute another person says or does something that is about to force you to reveal your true feelings, start coughing uncontrollably, explaining, "Please forgive me. I've had this horrible cough lately." As you cough, of course, you will have to close your eyes and lower your head, masking your feelings in the process.

Another way might be to make believe that you have something in your eye and to ask the other person to please help you out of this distressful condition. Or, in a dire emergency, it might be effective to suddenly close your eyes, as if in silent prayer. And still another way is to start scratching your forehead nervously, and in the process, lower your eyes so that the other person can't "read" them.

Such ploys tend to mask your real feelings, precluding the other person's being able to read you properly. At the same time, they lay the groundwork for your being able to use carefully thought out gestures and movements that can give *you*, not them, the advantage.

Time to counterattack

In a sense, you gain *some* psychic advantage simply by masking your real feelings, leaving the other person in the unenviable position of wondering precisely where you stand on the matter. Now, the idea is to "counterattack" — to throw your adversary off guard by using your own diversionary gestures, movements and tactics.

Again, being able to retaliate in this manner requires considerable practice and self-control, since you are now using body language in a studied rather than in a natural way.

For instance, let's assume you're the purchasing agent for a large company. You are negotiating with a salesman whose product your company wants very badly. In fact, you're unwilling to accept any other line.

Coping with power

This puts the salesman in a power position and gives him psychic advantage. But he has this advantage only if he *knows* how you feel about his product.

Certainly you're not going to *tell* the salesman you strongly prefer his product — at least not *verbally*. But you can easily reveal this fact without saying a word, through gestures and movements, if you're not *prepared* for the situation.

For example, left to your natural resources, you would likely smile when he mentions the virtues of his product, nod agreement when he spells out the benefits, and otherwise give strong body reactions (like maybe grabbing for your pen when he shows the contract) to display your eagerness. The idea is to retaliate with gestures and movements that will throw the salesman off guard.

Giving the "wrong" impression

For example, instead of listening with rapt attention as the salesman makes a very strong point for his product, you might shrug your shoulders and look pensively into space. These gestures are almost certain to make the salesman wonder. "What did I say wrong?" Other disconcerting gestures, such as making a telephone call in the middle of his pitch or sending a message to your secretary, can be equally distracting.

The final blow might come when the salesman poses the closing question, "Well, is there any reason we can't get this order going today? Any reason at all?"

You have already laid the groundwork for a negative response. Thus, it should come as no surprise when you frown and, shaking your head slowly from side to side, say, "I'm not sure just now. I'll simply have to think it over. There are some others I'm interested in." Thus "threatened," the salesman might now be in the mood to give you a major price concession.

You gain psychic advantage

Who now has psychic advantage in this situation? You do, despite the fact that his is definitely the product you want. But remember, psychic advantage is yours for only so long as the other person *thinks* you're not interested. And he'll think this way only so long as you give him the appropriate *negative* gestures.

Your real feeling is, "Can I sign it right now?" Your body message is, "Are you kidding? I'm going to look around first."

Again, the idea is to confuse others by masking your own feelings and then countering with gestures and movements that will give the other person just the opposite impression.

It's like playing poker

In this respect, you are much like a master poker player, one who has just drawn to an inside straight — and missed! You must not only conceal this fact with a "poker face," but convey just the opposite idea (that you hit the straight) by calling the other person's bet and raising $5. If you're a skilled enough player, you can pull it off — some of the time.

Successfully invading the other's territory

Clearly tied in with — in fact, inseparable from — the subject of body language is what psychologists call *territorial imperative*. As mentioned previously, this is a rather fanciful term for "privacy."

For example, given your choice, where do you *tend* to sit when you go to church? Attend a seminar? Frequent your favorite restaurant? More than likely, you prefer to sit in your *favorite* spot.

Why you resent intrusion

And why is it that you normally resent it when someone puts his feet on your desk, puts his arm on your shoulder, or sits too close? Quite obviously, he's violating *your* territory, the space around you that you instinctively feel is yours.

Anthropologists say that we're much like animals in this respect. We tend to "stake out" our own territory, whether it be at work or at home or in our favorite public place. And here is the point: Being aware of this fact gives you tremendous opportunity to gain psychic advantage simply by knowing *how* and *when* to invade the other person's territory — and, as a matter of fact, when *not* to do so.

How Ronnie White succeeded

Ronnie White, a young accountant for an energy company, apparently knows a thing or two about gaining psychic advantage by invading another's territory. He rose from junior accountant to group supervisor in less than four years.

One of his favorite tactics is to stage most meetings and confrontations in the *other* person's office. At first blush, meeting in another's office might seem to nullify the "home field" advantage for you.

Art of making impromptu visits

Not so, according to Ronnie. "In the first place," he says, "I usually manage to pop in unexpectedly. This throws the other person off guard and puts me at an advantage. You see, I've thoroughly planned what I want to say, and he has to improvise as the interview goes along.

"When I think I can get away with it, I charge right into the other person's office and sit where *I* will be most comfortable. For example, I've found that sitting on the corner of the other person's desk gives me a height advantage and more control over the interview."

Other subtle approaches

Ronnie often finds more subtle ways to further invade the other person's domain. These include using not-intended-to-be-used ashtrays, putting his feet on a table or desk, and perhaps taking off his coat and throwing it over a piece of furniture.

Ronnie's strategy in this respect is seemingly well founded, since you'll recall in an earlier chapter on *power* that most executives have their offices so arranged that it puts them in a dominant position. This puts visitors in a subordinate position and gives the occupant greater control.

How does Ronnie know whose desk he can sit on and whose desk he cannot occupy? He claims it's largely a matter of trial-and-error. But he also points out that it's an intuitive know-how that people like himself, who have a real feel for gaining psychic advantage, seem to possess.

Whom can he invade

Ronnie can usually tell after one incursion whether or not he'll be able to gain psychic advantage by successfully invading the other person's territory. "If they don't complain the first time, or if they remonstrate only mildly, I feel confident my strategy will work," he says. "In fact, the more passive the other party is, the more liberties I tend to take."

In extreme cases, Ronnie admits to using the other person's telephone, secretary, wash room, ash tray, and other items normally reserved strictly for the occupant.

Ronnie says there's one other prime advantage to inviting himself to the other person's bailiwick. "I can leave whenever I feel like it," he says, "since I'm the visitor. When they come to my office, *they* have this advantage."

Using "invisible agreements"

Ronnie is using a principle that is at work in every walk of life — the principle of the *invisible agreement*. Simply stated, this means that if another person permits you to take these liberties with him or his properties, he is, in effect, signing a "contract" that says it is perfectly all right for you to do so. He has given tacit permission.

Ronnie goes about as far as he can go in signing invisible agreements. The further he goes, the greater the degree of psychic advantage he seems to gain.

Once Ronnie finds he can successfully invade another's territory, he continues to do so at every possible turn, even when socializing or at lunch.

Keeping up the pressure

At lunch, for example, people have a tendency to stake out their "part" of the table. Realizing this, Ronnie keeps up his subtle campaign to gain psychic advantage by gradually moving his cigarettes or salad bowl — or whatever — over into the other person's side of the table.

At social events, Ronnie tends to burrow in within two or three feet of other people, clearly violating the unwritten social "law" that says, "Don't get too close; you're invading my privacy."

In most business transactions, the generally accepted "safe" distance between parties is five to ten feet. If you get closer than this, you're invading the other person's territory.

But some men, and particularly some women, use this knowledge to a great advantage in business negotiations. A saleslady whom we shall call Helen (since she doesn't want her real name used here) uses this technique with signal success.

How Helen does it

Helen sells franchises for a line of cosmetics. The company's *modus operandi* is to hold hotel meetings in which inspirational speakers tout the product and then invite the participants to stay over for private consultation with company representatives, including Helen.

Many of the would-be investors are men, and these are the ones Helen is primarily interested in.

Helen uses a small flip chart to explain the financial intricacies of the franchise contract, and to do so she sits directly in front of, and fairly close to, the prospect.

When she crosses her shapely legs and begins her sales spiel, it's a tossup as to which the would-be investor is more interested in, the program or the attractive saleslady who has just invaded his territory.

As if this invasion were not enough, Helen has another little gimmick she uses to gain psychic advantage if she doesn't seem to be getting the desired reaction. She manages to drop her pen so that it stops right in front of the prospect. When she hastily picks it up, she very gently brushes past his leg. This makes the invasion complete and often is the gesture that clinches the deal.

How to read and use body types

There's still another way to control people through body language, or perhaps body *knowledge* is the better word. And Jim Brown, a Dallas insurance executive, is a prime example of how to use a technique called *body-watching*. Obviously, there's nothing new about this pastime, but there *is* in the way Jim applies it.

Jim is now a successful insurance salesman. But it wasn't always that way. In fact, he did so poorly his first year that he almost went back to clerking. But Jim soon began to realize, as many others have in the selling game, that you don't sell insurance policies, you sell people, people who come in all sizes — short, tall, skinny, fat, and what have you. And it is precisely this point — the body build — that tells Jim how to handle a particular client.

Misjudging the professor

For example, early in his career, Jim was trying to sell a life policy to an anthropology professor at Southern Methodist University. Jim painted a vivid mental picture of what would happen if the young professor were accidentally to pass away in his prime, with his family in its formative stage. It was a rather eloquent, even emotional, appeal, and everything he said was true.

But the professor would have no part of it. He listened passively, giving Jim no clue as to his feelings. He asked few questions. And when Jim finished, the professor said simply, "Mr. Brown, do you realize that the odds are two million to one against such an eventuality?"

From this experience, Jim concluded — correctly in this case — that before people will buy insurance, they must be shown statistically how it will benefit them. And so, he vowed to try a "statistical" approach on his next prospect, who happened to be a former offensive lineman for the Dallas Cowboy pro football team.

Selling the "big guy"

Jim came up with a statistically impressive presentation, complete with charts, graphs, and actuarial data. Based on his experience with the anthropology professor, Jim figured he should have a cinch deal.

But it didn't materialize. The ex-football player actually

seemed somewhat bored with the sales pitch. At the end, he said, "Well, it sounds good. Let us think it over, and we'll give you a ring." Which meant, no sale.

A lesson learned

Knowing what he knows today, Jim would have treated these two prospects in an entirely different manner based to a large extent on the knowledge he now has about body structure.

The professor was tall and slender, with long hands and feet — somewhat the artistic type. The football player was a giant of a man, well over six feet and weighing in at about 265 pounds. Like many former players who had gotten away from the rigorous training grind, he had started to put on pounds around the middle.

So what do all these vital statistics mean? Plenty, to a body-watcher like Jim.

Slender people want proof

"Generally," he says, "I've discovered that slender people like the professor are usually the brainy type. They're thinkers and, as such, analyze things very carefully. Little wonder, then, that the professor was not overly impressed with my 'emotional' sales pitch. He's the kind who likes to see proof — you know, actuarial reports and this sort of thing.

"Now the football player was just the opposite — happy-go-lucky and people-oriented. I guess you could say he would be inclined to buy more on emotion. So you see, this is where I should have appealed to his sense of security and his family's well-being, rather than using the factual presentation I used."

Obviously, all people don't fit conveniently into one of these two extreme categories. In fact, most fall somewhere in between.

What about "in-betweens?"

"These people can have tendencies of both the stout and the slender types," Jim said. "But if you observe and listen carefully, you can usually see which way they lean."

For example, Jim once sold a large policy to an executive of average build who was slender but well developed. Jim was forced to use all the ammunition in his arsenal and appeal to both "sides" of his client's personality.

Doesn't all this add up to stereotyping people? "Perhaps to a degree it does," Jim says, "but it works for me most of the time, so I'd have to say it gives me a definite advantage."

Pursuing postural echo

Jim, who obviously is a very observant fellow, has also learned to gain a certain degree of control over people and situations by empathizing with others by assuming nearly identical body postures. It's a technique called *postural echo*, and it works like this.

When Jim is in a meeting where the boss — or the person in a power position — assumes a certain position, Jim assumes roughly the same position, subtly of course. For example, if the leader were to put his foot on a chair, thrust this elbow on his leg, and rest his chin on his thumb and forefinger, Jim would wait a few seconds and then assume roughly the same position.

Bellying up to the bar

Let's say that Jim is bellying up to the bar with a client. The client, as he talks, leans comfortably on his left elbow, puts his foot on the rail, and surveys the surroundings. Jim follows suit shortly thereafter, surveying the place in the same manner and from an almost identical position.

What's the advantage of all this? Well, Jim — and some psychologists — claim that assuming such "sympathetic" positions is a valid way of establishing rapport with the other person. It might be because imitation is still considered one of the highest forms of flattery.

Whatever the reason, Jim feels it works to help him gain control of situations, and eventually the people involved.

KEY IDEAS

Reading not only *body language* but also *body types* has become an increasingly important part of the communication process.

Psychic advantage practitioners can use a variety of techniques to read others' actions, or, defensively, to mask their own emotions, including:

- *Coding and decoding others' messages*
  - Learn to interpret basic gestures and movements.
  - Use this knowledge to gain advantage.
- *Masking your emotions, unmasking others'*
  - Interpret standard actions.
  - Hide your true feelings; send out facial false alarms.
  - Perfect diversionary tactics.
- *Invading another's territory*
  - Intrude on the other's privacy politely.
  - Write "invisible agreements."
- *Reading and using body types*
  - Learn to read body builds.
  - Use postural echo.

10

A Simple Shortcut
To Psychic Advantage

It's easy enough to see how you can *talk* your way to psychic advantage over others. But, paradoxically, you can gain just as much control — in some cases even more — by wisely practicing the other side of the coin, listening. Yes, listening! In fact, in some situations, it is the *best* way to gain control over others.

One of the reasons listening can be an effective shortcut to psychic advantage is that so few people listen well. Why? Well, one reason is that it has long been a neglected skill. Only in the past couple of decades or so has anyone really paid much attention to it. This despite the fact that managers, according to one reputable authority, spend as much as 45 percent of their time listening to others.

How people listen

Researchers within the past couple of decades have discovered that the average listening rate is four times the average speaking rate on routine material. That is, *you can listen roughly four times faster than others talk*. This gives you mental time on your hands, so to speak. And being relatively unversed in how to use this "spare" time, you engage in such nonproductive activities as daydreaming, wool-gathering, and other bad listening habits.

If what experts say is true (and most of us know in our heart of hearts that it is so), we typically fail to really listen to a great deal of what others say. In so doing, we fail to pick up valuable bits of information that *could* enable us to gain control of the situation and, of course, the people involved.

One authority has estimated that we're bombarded with about 2,000 messages a day. We probably "pick up" a fourth of these in helter-skelter style. The idea is to sharpen your listening skills to the point where you can zero in on *the* messages that will enable you to gain the upper hand in dealing with others.

How do you do this? Mainly by listening *actively* rather than passively, by shifting gears mentally as others talk — all the while analyzing, evaluating, and criticizing. In other words, be really *listening to* rather than simply *hearing* what others say.

The benefits of effective listening

Becoming a truly efficient listener can make you a rarity among your fellows. The good listener can become:

- A highly sought after "conversationalist" (Just try it and see.)
- A person who is thought of as knowledgeable and professional
- Highly popular at social events
- Adept at "controlling" conversations, since you get others to commit themselves

The techniques we'll use to improve listening skills are:

- Listening between the lines
- Listening aggressively
- Encouraging others to talk

Let's discuss these three techniques in some detail.

Listening between the lines

Two psychiatrists walking down the street were approached by a stranger who said, "Good morning." After the stranger passed, one psychiatrist said to the other, "What did he mean by that?"

Most of us aren't as analytical as psychiatrists, but we do "listen between the lines." Consciously, and perhaps to a greater extent unconsciously, we are constantly interpreting what others say. Or at least we *should,* for communication is a complex process that goes far beyond the words uttered by others.

Sometimes, of course, words can be taken at face value. For example, if you ask a seller what he wants for his home and he answers matter of factly, without changing expression or emphasizing any particular words, "Well, it's listed for $50,000," you can more or less accept this as pretty much of a statement of fact.

Best salesman, best listener

Sales, strangely enough, has emerged as one of the chief fields in which listening has belatedly been recognized as a prime asset. The successful salesman today is more likely to be a "fast listener" than a "fast talker."

Paul Bloxom, a veteran all-purpose salesman from Houston who has won more than his share of honors in "the good old days," hastens to concede the point.

"When I broke into the sales field 35 years ago, people generally thought of the typical salesman as a glib talker," he said. "And make no mistake, being able to talk effectively will always be an important part of his makeup.

Why clients are more sophisticated

"But, yes, I'd have to agree. Today's customers are, as a rule, more sophisticated, and most of them are quite articulate themselves. They're less inclined to go for a fast sales spiel; in fact, most of them would rather be talking themselves."

To verify the point, Paul reviewed his salesman-of-the-month winners for the past year. The name that stuck out most was Bill Prothero, a quiet and unassuming sort of guy who would probably have been voted "least likely to succeed" by his sales-training class.

How Bill does the job

"Bill surprised everyone, including myself," Paul said. "Here was a guy who didn't score particularly high on his sales-aptitude test. And he didn't exactly shine in role-playing during company training sessions.

"But within three months after he got in the field, Bill was winning salesman-of-the-month awards," he said. "And he hasn't stopped since."

How does Bill do it? Consensus among his fellow salesmen is that he somehow manages to maintain a high degree of empathy with his customers. In other words, he's able to see things from *their* point of view.

Empathy through listening

"I guess what it narrows down to," Paul said, "is that Bill is able to find out what the customer's problems are and then help them solve them. And when you stop and think about it, the only way you can really find out what the customer's problem is — is to listen well."

Is this a trend? Very likely. My guess is that the top salesmen in almost any company are articulate enough all right. But their strong suit is being able to listen — and listen well.

In this sense, then, there's little doubt that one can certainly listen one's way to psychic advantage.

Finding hidden messages

But most of us communicate extensively through inflection — the stress we put on particular words. Such messages are usually there in abundance. We simply have to be prepared to *listen* for them. Once you learn to "decode" such messages and use them to your advantage, you are on your way to gaining psychic advantage over the sender of such messages.

For example, had the above seller been willing to sell for under $50,000, there's a good chance he would have said, "Well, it's *listed* at $50,000." The emphasis on *listed* is for a purpose — to inform you that he'll consider a lower offer.

This same seller could have communicated the same message in still another way, by using certain facial gestures and body movements. For example, he could have said, "Well, it's listed at $50,000" and at the same time shrugged his shoulders and raised his eyebrows as if to say, "But who knows what'll happen if you make me a lower offer."

In fact, we communicate so continuously through kinesics, or *body language* as it's popularly called, that the topic was discussed fully in the preceding chapter.

In this section, however, we are concerned mainly with the *words* and *phrases* people use in everyday conversation. If you learn to perceive the hidden meanings these words convey, you can literally *listen* your way to psychic advantage.

Interpretation is personal

Interpreting the words and phrases others use is largely an individual matter. There are no universally accepted meanings, since it depends on *how* and by *whom* — and of course under what circumstances — the words are used. However, certain words and phrases do *tend* to have certain general meanings.

For example, I have noticed that some people use certain pet phrases over and over again. The question is, do such phrases merely represent a speaking habit, or do they reflect the user's frame of mind? I feel that in a great number of cases, they reflect the user's real, and often hidden, meaning.

Using an accentuator

These phrases generally fall into groups, one of which I call *accentuators*. This group includes opening words or phrases such as *honestly, in reality, truthfully, really, actually, to tell the truth,* and so forth.

True, on occasion, we all use these words literally. For instance, a woman says, "To tell the truth, I do not like that man." In this case, *to tell the truth* genuinely accentuates the fact that she really doesn't care for the guy.

But the same expression, in many other cases, belies the speaker's real feelings. For instance, a native Californian says, "To tell the truth (or truthfully), I'd rather live in New York any day than in Los Angeles."

Believe it or not

Why did the Californian use the accentuator *to tell the truth* before expressing his preference? If his motives were "pure" and his feelings sincere, why didn't he simply say, "I'd rather live in New York than Los Angeles"?

The more you learn to pick up and properly analyze these accentuators, the more readily you'll be able to tell whether the speaker is sincere or hiding his real feelings. Once you feel that he's concealing something, you can look for ways to gain psychic advantage.

For example, in this instance, the speaker was applying for a job with a New York company. Naturally it "sounded good" for him to prefer living in New York, a fact that a sharp personnel man would have likely picked up and used to his advantage.

Finding other hidden meanings

Here are a few other accentuators and the real meaning they sometimes hide:

"*Honestly,* we'll buy from you when we finally *do* decide to buy." Translation: "Your price is way out of line. We'll check with you later. Much later!"

"*In reality,* the company financial position is very good." Translation: "Aside from the fact that we're going to lose $10 million this year, we're in great shape financially."

"*Actually,* we'll be glad to come." Translation: "Much as we hate it, we'll be there."

Making out with minimizers

Another group of phrases consists of *minimizers*. These are phrases that are studiously calculated to *play down* people or situations — for one reason or another. Perhaps the most frequently heard minimizers are *incidentally, by the way, oh yes, before I forget, I just thought of something.*

To be sure, the minimizer can be a signal that what the speaker is about to say is a legitimate postscript, a bona fide parenthetical remark. But more often than not, it means just the opposite. The remark is not a postscript at all; it's a signal that the remark to follow is very important. So important, in fact, that the speaker is trying to slough the fact off in cavalier manner. Once you realize this, you can use this information to gain the upper hand in the transaction.

Minimizers in action

Here are a few examples of how minimizers work:

"*Incidentally,* we'd like to have your department help in this matter if you can find the time." Translation: "If you guys don't give us a hand, we're sunk."

"*Oh, yes,* I almost forgot to mention, we do have a few fringe benefits that will be of interest to you." Translation: "The salary's not much, but if you can live on fringe benefits, you're in luck."

"*I just thought of something,* why don't we make a big playroom out of the garage." Translation: "I've already checked with the contractor. It'll only cost $8,000 to do the work."

Looking for leaders

Then there are the group of words and phrases I call *leaders.* Others use them in an attempt to lead *you* to *their* position. Frequently used leaders are *needless to say, am I right in saying, you won't believe this, but, as you know, it goes without saying.*

Again, the purpose of such expressions quite frequently is to condition your thinking, to beg agreement. *As you know* is one of the most frequently used leaders.

For example, you can take the offensive and say to an associate, "*As you know,* Sam, we've felt all along that your company offers the best service in the business." Sam isn't likely to disagree, since he feels flattered. And why be disagreeable with someone who shares the same views? Thus, you gain a small degree of psychic advantage.

Being defensive

No, what you must constantly guard against is the usage of this effective *leader* against you. When you suspect that others are using the strategy to go one-up on you, learn to use effective counter strategems. For example, you might respond, "Why no, I didn't know that at all. As a matter of fact, I've been wondering about that situation for some time."

Looking at other leaders

"*Needless to say,* we'll want your recommendation on this matter before we take action." Translation: "We're going to vote this way, but go ahead and give us your thinking for the record."

"*Am I right* in saying that the new boss is an authoritarian leader?" Translation: "I am *dead right* in saying that he's a tyrant."

"*It goes without saying* that we're all going to ratify the new union agreement." Translation: "If you oppose the new agreement, you're in a heap of trouble."

Psychic advantage through pronouns

Our language abounds with countless other words and phrases that are used, often subconsciously, to gain some control over others' thought processes. For example, how a person uses pronouns often reflects a great deal about his personality and true feelings.

People who use "I" excessively, for instance, are generally highly egoistic, while people who use "we" are inclined to be more democratic. What you must be on guard against is the person who habitually uses neither "I" nor "we," but "it."

Stella's case

For example, Stella Stevens has become quite adept at "it." She will say, "*It* is generally felt that the new incentive plan will work well if it's properly presented."

Sounds innocent enough, but what Stella is doing — and you must detect this if you are to maintain control of her and the situation — is passing the buck.

For instance, what if the incentive plan doesn't work? What if it falls flat? Is Stella's judgment then questioned? Of course not. After all, Stella didn't give *her* opinion — "it" did. And "it" can represent just about anyone Stella wants it to represent. It was probably her administrative assistant who gave her the bad information in this case. By and large, "it" users manage to maintain a fairly high degree of psychic advantage in most of their relations.

Watch out for "Just a..."

Some attention ought to be paid to the "*Just a...*" group. "I'm just a housewife," "I'm just a worker here," or "I'm just a one-man department."

Sometimes such statements do reflect a poor self-image. But more often than not, the speaker is saying, "I'm really very important, but no one, including you, seems to think I am."

How do you use this knowledge to your benefit? Well, the first step obviously is to become a more perceptive listener, to determine when people mean what they say and when they actually are saying just the opposite. Once you've gained this insight, you can "counterattack" and gain control of the situation.

An advertising executive says, "We feel we can offer you many advantages. For one thing, we have a stronger art department than any other agency in the city. And our writers are great, too. They've won a bunch of awards for their creative works. *And incidentally,* we offer a strong public relations capability along with our regular services."

Judgment takes over

At this point, you exercise your ability to perceive his true meaning. Does the "incidentally" mean that he just happened to think of the public relations service as a sort of postscript? Or does he have an ulterior motive?

Assuming you feel reasonably certain that "incidentally" is a ploy, the idea is to now bring the real meaning out into the open and to gain psychic advantage in the negotiation.

You might say, "Well, Mr. Jones, I'll agree with you that your people do good creative work. But now about that public relations service. That idea really appeals to me. You know, we've got lots of things going on around here that would make good press. But tell me, isn't this really an "extra" for you? I mean, don't you charge extra for this kind of public relations service?"

"Well, not really. That is, it's all included in the package cost."

The moment of truth

"But that does put your *price* a little above the other bidders. So this means that in reality, we would be paying for the so-called 'free' service."

"Well, yes, in a manner of speaking. But the point is —
it really is superior service."

"If we were to give you the contract, would you make
your price competitive with the other bidders and still throw
in the public relations service?"

"You drive an awful hard bargain. But yes, for *your*
business, I'll throw in the PR service for free."

"It's a deal."

Thus perceptive listening has gained you control of the
situation, and psychic advantage over the advertising account
executive.

Listening aggressively

Reggie Brown is a typical office know-it-all. You know
the kind — he can talk on just about any subject at the drop of
a hat. Unfortunately, Reggie *is* a learned and interesting fellow, a fact that makes it quite easy for him to gain psychic
advantage in conversation with others. Here, for example, is an
excerpt from one of Reggie's office dissertations on "foreign
policy."

How to dazzle with statistics

"Well, I personally think we are on a par with the Rus-
sians, and maybe even slightly ahead. You see, it's true that
Russia has us outnumbered in intercontinental ballistics mis-
siles: 2,235 to 1,650. But you see, that doesn't tell the whole
story. Our ICBMs carry a bigger warhead, giving us overall
about seven percent more efficiency per missile. Furthermore,
our ICBMs are ten percent more accurate."

Now this sort of statistical stuff, coupled with Reggie's
erudite appraisal of the nation's foreign policy, does indeed
make his words ring with a certain authority. It sounds impres-

sive, and as a matter of fact, is. So, the net effect is that it gives Reggie psychic advantage over others in the conversation. You, of course, can gain this same advantage by developing this same kind of conversational expertise.

But the big problem is, how do you *defense* this sort of thing and thus gain greater control?

Avoiding confrontations

The first step is to *listen* carefully to the other person's rationale, to the *basis* for his line of reasoning. Then, to the attack.

To be sure, you'll want to avoid a head-on confrontation. To question another undiplomatically makes you the "heavy" and will force others to side with your adversary. It would further brand you as being argumentative and rude.

Buffer statement helps

So before you launch your critique, serve up a "buffer statement" to soften your response. The buffer can be something like, "Well, Reggie, that's an extremely interesting observation. It's refreshing to hear a real student of military and foreign policy." Then, just as Reggie begins to savor his supremacy, you attack! "But by the way, do you mind my asking, where did you get those figures about the ICBMs?"

Reggie could answer in one of several ways, any one of which probably puts him solidly behind the eight ball and gives you an opening to gain psychic advantage.

He could, for example, say, "Why, I read it in the *Evening Times.*" Whereupon you question, "Was it a by-line story? Just who was the author?" If he quotes what seems to be a reliable and credible source, you can always counter with,

"That's interesting, because only recently I read in the (quote your own reliable source) that the ratio was considerably less, more like 2,250 to 1,750." This way, you are not attacking him, just his *source*.

A legal maxim applies

In law there is a maxim that goes, "That which can be stated without proof, can be denied without proof." This means simply that if Reggie cannot back up his statement, he "loses" and you win. What do you win? Psychic advantage, of course.

The worst thing Reggie can do is to quote no source at all. In this case, it becomes obvious that it is *his* answer. Then all you have to do is establish that Reggie is not a military expert who is privy to government archives. A simple little query like, "I suppose you have access to official Russian and U.S. figures or papers on this?" ought to prove the point nicely. He is the same as "discredited." You "win."

Why experts have an advantage

Think back now. Why do people like teachers, preachers, coaches, doctors, lawyers, and others normally have strong psychic advantage over most of us? Because they are in a position of constantly doling out *advice*. They are assuming the role of the expert; we are the "students." Thus they are logically in the "driver's seat."

Advantage conceded

No doubt, we must usually concede this advantage in teacher-student, preacher-congregation, boss-subordinate relationships, or at least in most of them, to keep the relationship on an even keel. To gain psychic advantage in many of these instances, even if you could, would reflect adversely on your image.

But these relationships are the exception. By and large, most of your dealings will be with superiors, peers, or subordinates in the business world, and depending on the circumstances, this is where you will want to exert yourself and gain the upper hand.

You can do so by questioning their authority (and source) as done in the previous example. Or, you can gain psychic advantage by (1) preventing them from hogging the conversation or (2) failing to yield to their commands, ultimatums, and other bullying tactics.

Not letting them hog the conversation

If another tends to hog the conversation, we more or less "concede" that they are smarter and more aggressive than we; thus, they build up psychic advantage throughout the conversation. The solution is clearly to take action that will wrest the conversation from him — to get him off center stage.

One way is to hog the conversation yourself, using some of the techniques discussed in Chapter 7. Another is to use tactics ideally suited to your personality. I have found two that are especially effective — interrupting periodically, especially on minor points, and taking notes as the other person talks.

The art of interrupting

Interrupting, as mentioned previously, is somewhat of an art within itself. The idea is to interrupt gracefully so as not to appear rude and gain resentment from others. Again, a good buffer statement like, "I don't mean to interrupt, but..." will usually do the trick.

Such interruptions, to be most effective, should be on

relatively minor issues. Speakers will find this extremely distracting, since they are attempting to make a point that they consider to be a key issue. For example, let's assume your conversational partner is discussing some weighty issue such as the decline of the Third Reich from a historical point of view. The idea is to wait for a "break" in the conversation, such as when the talker takes a drag off a cigarette, and interject, "I don't mean to interrupt, Hal, but you know your talking about Germany reminds me of something I found out when I was over there. Do you realize most Germans drink their beer at room temperature? If I might take just a moment, let me tell you about the time I was in Stuttgart. You see..." and off you go.

You have interrupted gracefully, and you have, in a fashion, stayed on the subject. I have found that after two or three such interruptions, the speaker will tend to become totally exasperated and give up in disgust. This gives you the floor, and in the process, psychic advantage over the other person.

Note-taking distracts

The next time you're being psyched out by a long-winded expert, try this little experiment. Pull out a little notebook, wrinkle your brow as if trying to make a profound judgment, and then write down — or *appear* to write down — a few notes.

Make certain, of course, that the talker is *un*able to *see* your notes, especially if you're only pretending to write something down. Repeat the process every time the expert appears to make an "unusual" remark — one that commits him to a position or course of action.

For example, I was once engaged in conversation with a vice president of a large insurance company. The executive was pontificating at length about a diversity of subjects (holding complete control, I might add) and finally started taking shots at the Insurance Commission.

Stopping a tirade

He became increasingly radical. As he did so, I whipped out my little notebook, jotted down a couple of items, placed the notebook in my pocket, and then resumed a rapt listening posture. The first two times I did this slowed him down only slightly. It was the third time, right after he said, "The Insurance Commissioner is a knucklehead, and I know for a fact that he takes kickbacks," that the executive was stopped cold, right in the middle of his tirade.

"What in the world are you writing down?" he asked.

"Oh, not much," I explained casually. "You see, I'm a free-lance writer. I make it a habit to jot down interesting things that I see and hear from time to time."

"Oh," he said. "Well, just so you don't quote *me*."

I simply smiled noncommitally. What was the result of all this? The note-taking not only stopped his tirade, but subdued him throughout the rest of the conversation. He did get cranked up briefly once again, but at this point I just took out my notebook and *appeared* to take "notes." He stopped again.

Why the technique works

The reason the tactic works so well is that most people aren't willing, in most cases, to risk seeing their words in print.

Most of us speak off the cuff most of the time, realizing that our remarks will never be extensively critiqued. It is the *threat* that such remarks will be put up for public scrutiny that makes note-taking such a potent weapon in gaining conversational psychic advantage.

Encouraging others to talk

You obviously can't listen if the other person isn't talking. Someone has said that God gave you two ears and one mouth so that you could listen twice as much as you talk. The point here is that the more you can get the other person to talk, the more likely you are to get him to reveal his true feelings.

In conversation, the other person potentially has an "advantage" over you in that he can carefully choose the words and ideas that will fit *his* ends. In order to regain psychic advantage in such cases, you must combine sharp listening skills with adroit questioning techniques to gain control of the situation.

There are at least two effective ways of doing this: Get the other person to *elaborate* or get him to *clarify*. Those who master these two techniques can become amazingly adept at getting the *real* story from others.

How Roger uses elaboration

Elaboration is a technique used expertly by Roger Lindstrom, an executive placement counsellor. In this capacity, Roger must frequently dig for the *real* facts about applicants, who understandably want to put their best foot forward. But in order to do so, they must frequently omit past events or personal idiosyncrasies that might not reflect favorably.

Roger is in a power position, of course, by being able to recommend whether to hire. But the applicant is not without leverage himself, since he can carefully "edit" his own words in the interview to create the desired impression. The only way Roger can gain clear psychic advantage in such cases is to make sure he gets the *full* facts from the applicant, including those the applicant hadn't intended to give. This is a job that only skilled interviewers such as Roger are able to pull off.

Three-step process

There are really three steps in this interview process:

1. Get the applicant — or whoever — to talk freely.
2. Interpret his words in the light of what appears to be the case.
3. Look for and try to expose hidden meanings or omitted facts.

"The key to my getting the real information I need is based on two factors — the ability to listen well and the ability to ask the right questions," Roger said. "The questions need not be difficult. In fact, the technique works much better if they are sort of 'mini-questions' — just enough to show I'm paying attention and to keep the applicant talking." The principle is illustrated in the following interview.

The interview

"How long have you been on the job?" Roger asks the applicant.

"About ten years," the applicant responds confidently. His manner of responding indicates to Roger that the applicant is proud of his work record.

"That's a pretty good record," Roger responds. "Any particular reason for wanting to change?"

The faint smile on the applicant's face turns into a slight frown. This reaction leads Roger to feel that the applicant is carefully considering his responses — possibly even about to fabricate a story.

Real meaning emerges

"Well, mainly because I need more money," the applicant says. "There are a few other reasons, but mainly it's money."

"Other reasons?"

"Well, yes, but they're sort of minor. Nothing, really."

"Minor?"

"Yes. Well, one of the reasons I'm quitting my present job is because my boss has frankly got it in for me."

"Got it in for you?"

"Yeah. He's active in a lot of company activities, like the Red Cross drive, the Recreation Association, the Management Club, and this sort of thing, and he wants me to be just as active as he is. But you see, I sort of feel my time is my own. I get paid for doing my job, and I do it well. But when it comes to this extracurricular stuff, I draw the line. This and that other stuff."

"Other stuff?"

"Well, he's also sort of a nut on education. Always wanting us to attend seminars put on by the company — and outside, too."

"But won't these seminars help you on your job?"

"A little, maybe. But it's the idea of *having* to attend that really bugs me."

How Roger gains control

The interview continues in this vein for some time. Who is in control? The applicant appears to be, since he's doing most of the talking. But the *real* control is in the hands of Roger, who has skillfully guided the conversation along paths he wanted it to take.

How? By listening intently and asking just enough brief questions ("Other reasons?" "Minor?" "Got it in for you?" "Other stuff?") to keep the applicant talking.

On paper the applicant looks good. He has an MBA from an Ivy League school, ten years on the job, and excellent recommendations. But there is one major flaw as far as Roger is concerned.

The applicant has all the earmarks of being a nonconformist, a trait that is highly desirable in some instances, but not this one. Roger is frankly looking for an "organization man," someone who feels extracurricular activities are part of the job.

Thus, by controlling the interview, and the applicant, Roger saved himself — and the applicant — some embarrassing moments downstream.

Clarification as a key

Clarification is an equally effective technique for gaining control of people and situations. It, too, is based on the ability to listen well and to ask relevant questions.

Salespeople use this technique regularly to close transactions. Susan Blake, a real estate salesperson, elevated herself from failure to success in selling, thanks mainly to the clarification technique, which is based primarily on effective listening and questioning techniques.

Susan interviews a client

Here's Susan in action interviewing a client.

"What kind of home did you and Mrs. Smith have in mind?" Susan inquires.

"A three bedroom will do, maybe four, if the price is right," Mr. Smith says. "But three should do it. At least two baths. And this is assuming all this isn't too expensive."

"Too expensive?"

"Yes, I'd say not over $60,000."

"Very well, Mr. Smith. But as you know, you have the

financial strength to afford a more expensive home if you prefer."

Smith merely shrugs his shoulders and rolls his eyes upward.

"How about location?" Susan continues.

"We definitely prefer the southwest part of town," Mrs. Smith says, "and the area must be quiet. No traffic."

"How about the monthly payments?"

"We'd certainly like to keep them under $450."

"All right. Now tell me, would you consider an assumption?"

"A what?"

"An assumption. That is, you can assume someone else's loan, probably at a much lower interest rate."

"How much would that take?"

"Oh, probably anywhere from $10,000 to $25,000 for a really good buy. Does that sound reasonable to you?"

Smith does not answer directly. Instead, he says simply, "Mmmmm. Could be. We'll see."

Further questions from Susan reveal that the Smiths prefer fairly large bedrooms, a not-too-large yard, and plenty of closet space.

The "new" Susan takes over

The "old" Susan, the one-time failure in real estate, would have taken this information, and then showed the Smiths what *she* thought they should buy. She admitted to *hearing* without *listening* in those days.

But the "new" Susan, the successful real estate operative, really *heard* what this client said, and proved it at the closing transaction.

Like many prospects, the Smiths looked for several days and got hopelessly confused. They finally concluded, "Thanks for everything, but we want to think it over. We'll give you a call in a couple of days."

The new Susan knew from experience that clients who want to "think it over" rarely return. Thus, at this point, you can realistically say that she had lost control of the clients and the sale.

But here's where she used the clarification technique, stressing effective listening, to regain control and psychic advantage.

The questioning process

"Mr. and Mrs. Smith," she said, "I can understand your wanting to think it over. Buying property is one of the biggest decisions we have to make. However, my only purpose in being here is to help you make a wise decision, so do you mind my asking if it's the price you're concerned with?"

"Well, no, not exactly. It's a little bit higher than we wanted to pay. But as you said, we've got the financial strength to swing it."

"How about the down payment? Is it all right?"

"We can swing that, too."

"Location?"

"Yes, the location is fine."

"Are you concerned about the monthly payment?"

"A little, but no real problem there, either."

"How about the noise factor, Mrs. Smith. I noticed you looked a bit apprehensive when the jet flew over a moment ago."

"Well, yes, that did give me pause. Does that happen very often?"

"Not at all, only when the airport is using the auxiliary runway, and that's rarely. Tell you what, why don't we drop by a couple of other homes in the areas and see if any of the owners are bothered by the airplane noise."

Neighbors react favorably

In this particular case, Susan was reasonably sure she would get a "favorable" response to most of her questions, since she had qualified the Smiths properly by really listening to their needs.

You would have to say that the ability to listen well and to use the clarification technique judiciously netted Susan psychic advantage — and the sale.

KEY IDEAS

Listening has long been one of the most neglected communication skills.

Today, however, people in all walks of life are finding that they can attain their goals — and psychic advantage — by:

- *Listening between the lines*
  - Learn to use and interpret inflection.
  - Discover how to "code" and "decode" messages.
  - Use words and phrases to your advantage.
  - Find out how to prevent "conversation hogging."
- *Listening aggressively*
  - Discover how to defuse the glib talker.
  - Ascertain the basis of his thinking.
  - Attack the cause, not the individual.
  - Cope with "advice-givers."
- *Encouraging others to talk*
  - Get others to elaborate.
  - Get others to clarify.
  - Discover their "editing" techniques.

11

How to Gain Psychic Advantage When You're The Underdog

Almost anyone can gain a degree of psychic advantage by combining a positive state of mind with the solid strategies discussed in this book.

Developing and using these strategies can be — in fact, often is — time consuming and, in many cases, most difficult. For these reasons you need to continually play over in your mind the tremendous benefits to be gained from developing psychic advantage.

Individuals with high psychic advantage can usually:

- Get ahead in their business or profession
- Develop a strong social position
- Maintain a high degree of self-confidence
- Hold their own in most transactions, even against those who show clear psychic advantage

It is this latter point that needs special attention. For regardless of how adept you become at gaining psychic advantage, you'll always be running into people who will have an advantage over you. In other words, you'll continue to be the *underdog* in many of your dealings with others. After all, there are many more "Indians" than "chiefs."

And let's face it, the underdog *does* usually lose. Sure, David slew Goliath. But that was an exception. The "favorite" usually wins out because of superior skill.

So what can you do to either gain parity, or possibly even come out on top, when you're in the underdog role? You can learn to:

- Use the 4-P approach.
- Act with supreme confidence.
- Develop "equalizers."

Use the 4-P approach

I think that without doubt one of the best ways to even things up with a person who has psychic advantage over you is to exhibit what I call the 4-P approach. Show an unusually high degree of *pride, praise, preparation,* and *professionalism* in what you're doing.

Borrowing from a bank

For example, trying to borrow a large sum of money from a bank with only limited collateral is a tough proposition. The banker has clear psychic advantage in this case. Thus it's an ideal situation for the 4-P approach.

John Reese, a Texas developer, found himself in this situation many times during the early days of his meteoric business career — big ideas and little cash. He learned to use the 4-P approach to near perfection.

"I prepare myself for the interview by trying to put myself in the banker's shoes," Reese says. "He's got every advantage, of course, since he has the money, and obviously the power to arbitrarily turn me down if he so chooses.

Anticipating banker's questions

"Experience has taught me that the banker wants to know the answer to several basic questions. How much do I want and for how long? How do I plan to use the money, and specifically, how am I going to pay it back? In addition, how will I be able to pay off if my plan goes wrong?

· "So, instead of *waiting* for the banker to ask me these questions, and in the process control the interview, I launch right into my pitch shortly after we exchange amenities and establish the relationship.

"You see, if I wait for *him* to ask the questions, *he* controls the interview. I'm pretty much in the position of an 'applicant' asking for a 'job'.

How to take the initiative

"So, in order to offset this advantage he has — in other words, to reduce the *control* he exercises over the interview — I simply assume the initiative and more or less control the interview myself.

"Shortly after exchanging pleasantries, I say something like, 'Mr. Banker, my organization would like to buy a fast-food franchise that is moving into the area. As shown in our audited report, the system has done well on the West Coast and in the Midwest.

"We'd like to get the loan for 25 years. We plan to pay it back from earnings we get from the franchise. Our business volume is projected on what similar operations have done during their first five years in business. Here's our written projection on this program, which as you can see, has been audited by our accounting firm."

What has Reese proven?

Let's stop here and see what Reese accomplished with this onslaught of facts. Two things at least. First, he has shown that he has done his homework. He's thoroughly prepared, and this is the hallmark of a true professional. Second, he has set the tone and pace of the interview, you might say *controlled* it to a large extent. He's being treated like the entrepreneur that he is rather than a "job applicant."

So much for *preparation* and *professionalism*. How about the other two P's — *pride* and *praise?* Reese takes care of these in the interview and in the written report, and perhaps even more importantly, in his ability to socialize.

Homework reflects pride

"The pride you show in your work is reflected in the amount of homework you've done," Reese continues. "It relates directly to *character,* and with most bankers, this is probably the greatest single asset you have going for you. I'd say it counts as much as 50 percent in your getting the loan. Sure, they're interested in cash flow, market conditions, and all that. But primarily, they want to know if you're a solid citizen. So I spend as much time as I feel is necessary getting this point across — both in the interview and in the written proposal we give the banker."

That leaves the fourth P — *praise*. And this is where Reese usually provides the "clincher."

"Like most other business people, bankers are human," he points out. "They like to be called by their first names, and remembered on their birthdays and anniversarys and at Christ-

mas. And they're not adverse to being wined and dined, providing it's done above board and in good taste."

Wining and dining pays off

All this Reese does in lavish fashion and with consummate artistry.

"I'll try to pick up my banker about 11:15 and arrive at
the club no later than 11:45," Reese says, "just before the rush
starts. This way, I can get a corner table, which affords us more
privacy.

"This latter point is tremendously important, since it
eliminates many of the interruptions you normally get when you
arrive late and are bothered by both customers and waiters."

Preparation paves the way

Again, it is thorough *preparation* that paves the way for
a successful business luncheon or dinner. The point to remember here, Reese asserts, is that bankers and most other businessmen like to be remembered. "It's a form of praise," Reese says,
"and everyone loves praise."

This is the way Reese, the one-time underdog, learned
to gain a great deal of psychic advantage with bankers. This
treatment usually gets him what he asks for.

Still, because he is a real pro, Reese takes one final step
in his preparation. What if he gets the loan and his plan doesn't
work?

Devising an alternate plan

"I almost always work out an alternate plan," he says,
"just in case things don't work out as we expect. If the project

flops and I have to go back to the banker to get a new loan, I'm of course even more vulnerable to his power.

"So again, rather than wait for *him* to conduct the interview, I get my questions all lined up and try to gain the initiative in the interview."

One of the best ways to control an interview is to plan your questions beforehand and then ask them in a more or less impromptu fashion. Reese's second interview revolves around questions like these: "Harry, I have the feeling you're not going to renew my loan. May I ask, what would you do in my place? Maybe I should go to another bank? Which one? Who should I ask for at this bank? What should I tell him? Is it all right if I tell him there's been a change in policy at your bank? What do you plan to tell him?"

Reese is again controlling the interview. And if you will review the questions, you will find that he is getting the banker to tell him exactly how to solve his problem.

"You see," Reese says, "bankers are not only flattered by praise, they like to be put in the position of being able to help. If I get the answer to my questions, I know whom to approach and exactly how to approach them. In addition, I'll know what kind of report my original banker is going to give. Thus I have solid information on which to base my interview with the banker."

Put the 4-P formula (pride, praise, preparation, and professionalism) to work for you. It's a most effective way of enhancing your position when you're the underdog.

How to act with supreme confidence

If you're a "nice guy," you are likely to find yourself in the underdog role in many of your daily encounters. Most people have psychic advantage over you a great deal of the time.

While nice guys don't always finish last, they do often take their lumps when it comes to dealing effectively with others. Conversely, it's the "tough guy" who tends to dominate the scene in the business world.

Developing mental toughness

This doesn't mean you have to be built like, nor act like an NFL linebacker (though this is one clear way to psychic advantage). It does mean that you need to develop a *mental* toughness, the kind that characterizes most successful business and professional people.

Develop this kind of mental toughness, and you can say goodbye to being the perennial underdog, the proverbial door-mat. And how do you develop this mental toughness? By developing expertise in one or more of the following areas:

To succeed, act "as if"

Act "as if" you were in a position of authority. No one can convince Jack Osborne, a salesman of big-ticket items like boats and planes, that *imagination* isn't one of man's most cherished faculties. By using it more effectively, he elevated himself from obscurity — and a relatively low income — to a six-figure paycheck.

"My biggest problem," Jack admitted, "was one of ego, or should I say, lack of it. You see, most of my sales were to people with money.

Dealing with rich folk

"I usually felt like the poor guy talking to the rich guy, the dummy talking to someone of background and breeding. My sales had reached a low point when my sales manager called me in and said, 'Jack, your problem is that you're going to these people hat in hand. You act like they're doing you a favor just letting you talk to them. Hell, man, you've got a product they want and really *need.* So when in Rome, do it their way. All you have to do is to *act, talk,* and *dress* like you're one of them. Then, as one jet-setter to another, show them what they have to gain by dealing with you.'

"I felt like a fool doing this at first," Jack continued. "I mean, here I was nearly broke, and there I was...masquerading as a playboy. But after a while, I got more and more comfortable in the role, and today I *am* one of them in a manner of speaking. At least, they *feel* that way, and that's what's important."

Visualizing clients in the buff

Jack's case is not uncommon. Another salesman uses the same philosophy, only with a slightly different twist. He visualizes his really important clients as sitting across the table completely nude. "It's the greatest equalizer I've ever seen," he said.

So what's new about this strategy? Absolutely nothing. Hans Vaihinger set down the basic ideas a few generations ago in *The Philosophy of "As If."* The ideas are as good today as they were then.

I have found that the *as if* approach to psychic advantage works even better if you will base your attitude on a real success.

For example, try to remember the precise feeling you had following your last success, whether it was an ovation for a speech you gave or simply a compliment from your boss for completing a tough project on schedule. Then carry this feeling into your action.

What if you couldn't fail?

If you want to gain the upper hand in more of your relationships, do like Jack Osborne. Next time you get ready to swing a big deal or communicate with somebody of great importance to you, just sit down and ask yourself one question: *What would I be doing now, what position would I take, if I knew that it was impossible to fail?*

Then do it! Act *as if* it were impossible to fail. Like Jack, you can imagine your way to psychic advantage. It's a sound way to ascend from underdog to top banana.

Don't "poor boy" it

Don't be subservient to others. For years, Robert Stangl was a typical "yes man." He listened with rapt attention when his superiors spoke. He showed almost constant agreement, either verbally or with appropriate gestures — or both. And he overused such phrases as "yes sir" and "no sir," and the like.

Where did all of this get him professionally? One small step up the management ladder in five years.

It was at this point that Robert changed his "communications style." Except in rare cases, he dropped the "yes sirs" and "no sirs" and stopped clinging to the every word spoken by others, except when the situation obviously called for it.

Today Robert is in middle management and holds his own with superiors and peers alike.

How Robert got ahead

Does this suggest that rudeness pays off in the executive rat race, while politeness is passé? Not at all, according to Robert.

"I finally came to realize," he said, "that by my every action, I was building the other person up and putting myself in an inferior position. I didn't realize it, but I was using terms like 'yes sir' and 'no sir' habitually. I tried to justify excessive usage of such terms on the grounds that they were *polite*. But my business partner pointed out that they went beyond politeness; they were almost subservient.

"To confirm this idea, I began to observe more closely the speech habits and mannerisms of people in our own management structure. Not a single one used these terms excessively. For the most part, they used a simple 'yes' or 'no.' To a man — and yes, woman — they exhibited mental toughness, a hard-nosed approach to their business affairs.

"Mental" toughness is the answer

"To be sure, they had different leadership styles. Some were democratic, some authoritarian; some talked tough, others didn't. But the overall impression was one of *mental* toughness.

"Perhaps the action explains itself. It is hard to appear 'tough' while you are smiling condescendingly and saying 'yes sir' and 'no sir.' Mind you, I don't say that these phrases do not have their place. They obviously do. But I have found that a polite, but firm 'yes' or 'no' gets the job done and puts me on a par with whomever I'm talking to."

Can you listen too well?

As a further result of his study, Robert also changed his listening "style." "Don't get me wrong," he said, "being a good listener is tremendously important, especially to people in sales work. But in dealing with people in general, particularly superiors, I found that I was actually listening *too* well.

"You see, when you hang onto the other person's every word, when you show by your every gesture and response that you are listening to him as if his word were gospel, you are elevating his status and lowering yours. *He* gains psychic advantage.

Keeping the other party off balance

"To remedy this, I now try to keep the other person off balance a bit. I listen as carefully as ever; I just don't *show* it."

One of Robert's tactics is to show rapt attention for a period and then to suddenly let his eyes wander to something on the other person's desk or perhaps a picture on the wall. "I do this just often enough — and long enough — to let the other person know that I'm not totally wrapped up in his every word. This tends to keep him 'honest' and prevents him from gaining a high degree of control over me."

Be polite, but don't "hang on"

Robert also admits to being quite careful with whom and under what circumstances he uses the technique. "It depends entirely on the situation," he said. "Still, I've found that as a rule, the strategy works just as well with superiors as it does with peers and subordinates."

Be polite. Be firm. Be congenial. Just don't hang onto the other person's every word. In doing so, you increase your control over the interview and lessen the other person's chances of gaining psychic advantage in the relationship.

How to look and talk "tough"

Learn to look and talk "tough." (At least have the capability.) There's another technique Robert picked up in his study of successful people. If you want to show a position of power and dominion over others, it often helps to be able to *look* and *talk* tough. Again, we're talking about tough in the *mental* sense.

Tough talk is a tactic used by many superiors to lord it over subordinates and peers. They feel that the raunchier the language, the more powerful they become. This elevates them, and at the same time puts you down a notch.

Profanity as a tool

"I discovered this with my first boss," Robert said. "He was usually fairly temperate in his speech in public. But when he got a subordinate in his sights, one he wanted to impress with his position, it was "damn the torpedos and full steam ahead.""

Robert felt that his boss used profanity in such instances for a couple of reasons. One, of course, was to show clearly that he was in a power position. The other was because the boss was a bit insecure in his management role and used invective to show it.

Coping with cussin'

Thus, the superior who launches into a diatribe and gets little or no "resistance" from you is gaining clear psychic advantage, while you are being shoved deeper and deeper into the underdog position.

"By cussing and ranting in front of me," Robert said, "he was saying, 'I can talk to you any way I like because I'm in a position to do so, but you're not supposed to talk back this way to me.' So what did I do? I surprised him by retaliating with a few choice cuss words of my own.

"For example, he might say, 'I'm not gonna let any sonofabitch like that work in my shop.' To which I would respond, 'Right, you give those bastards an inch and they want a mile!' And so forth.

More members equals more profanity

"Now in conference, where several people are present, this sort of profanity invariably seems to escalate. They try to outcuss each other. But strangely enough, in most one-on-one situations, the act of retaliating with profanity of your own tends to tone the conversation down. Having done this, you have somewhat nullified his power play and have gained some control over the situation.

Forget Brando and Bogart

Looking tough is quite another matter. It does not necessarily mean walking around the office Humphrey Bogart style, with your hat brim turned down, trench coat collar turned up, and a cigarette dangling from the corner of your mouth. Nor does it mean wearing form-fitting T-shirts, à la Marlon Brando.

It does mean that you affect the demeanor of the typical executive who has the responsibility of the world on his shoulders. This look is familiar to most. It typically includes a furrowed brow, a slight scowl, a steady glare, and a mouth seemingly always turned down at the ends. Is this guy tough? How would *you* like to ask him for a raise or a business concession?

Developing "equalizers"

What would you do if you were attacked by a 275-pound brute? Very likely, you'd look for a beer bottle, baseball bat, two-by-four, or some equally lethal "equalizer." Otherwise, you'd likely get wiped out.

Obviously, you can't retaliate so violently when you're

"attacked" by your boss or others whose stature automatically casts you in the role of underdog. But if you make no effort at all to "keep up" with superiors, you soon get relegated to the role of perennial underdog — the old office doormat! To avoid this dilemma, you'll need to master some psychological equalizers — tactics that will put you not only on a par but one-up on your opposite number.

The two most effective equalizers I've seen used in the business world, and elsewhere for that matter, are developing extreme competence and using a third party. Let's discuss each.

On becoming "super competent"

Developing extreme competence. You might say that Jerry Grimes was a pronounced underdog in the marketing department of a major aerospace firm.

He did not own a college degree, as most of his co-workers did. He had been an enlisted man in the Air Force, whereas most of his associates had been staff-grade officers. He was average in intelligence and appearance, while many of his marketing cohorts were highly articulate and of outstanding demeanor.

Because of these facts, Grimes was cast in the role of "underdog," not only in dealing with customers, but in relating to all levels of employees within his own department. Still, Grimes had one thing going for him. He was *aware* of his shortcomings, and he had decided to meet head-on this problem of gaining some degree of control over his destiny.

Finding ways to impress

"At first I could see no way out at all," Grimes said. "Then it came to me while I was studying the plans for a sophisticated new bomber we had on the drawing boards.

"Like almost all new bombers of its type, this airplane was controversial. It occurred to me at this moment that the *one* way I could make myself invaluable to the company was to become not only an expert on this new model airplane, but on our nation's defense policies and posture as a whole. This way, I would be better prepared to 'cope' with clients and fellow workers alike."

How Grimes became an expert

Grimes did just that. He familiarized himself so thoroughly with the company's proposal that he could quote its capabilities almost as well as the chief design engineer. Then he became a veritable expert on the nation's defense policies, enabling him to make a persuasive case for the role his company's new bomber would play in the nation's defense.

Did Grimes gain psychic advantage as a result of all this? Indeed he did. In fact, when a Congressional investigation was launched the next year on whether the Air Force would order his company's plane or a competitor's, Grimes went to Washington as one of the company representatives to testify before a special committee.

Gaining extreme competence in a subject or task may not always be the fastest way to gain advantage over others, but it is certainly one of the *surest* methods. True, the technique almost always calls for hard work — and lots of it! But then, no one said this business of gaining psychic advantage, especially when you're a habitual underdog, would be easy.

How a woman gained psychic advantage

One other brief case illustrates the principle. It is cited here because, despite pious pronouncements of sexual equality, few women really make it big in business and industry, at least not in upper-level jobs.

A very talented — and significantly, very ambitious — lady we'll call Rhoda (she feels "publicity" would be rubbing salt in the wound) excelled at her job over a period of years. Her job was to solicit loans from real estate companies for her firm. Rhoda had recently set a record volume for her company for a one-year period.

Despite her record, Rhoda was consistently bypassed for promotion to the company's board of directors. Others with lesser production records (and yes, they were men) were elevated to the top spots.

Coping with a "chauvinistic pig"

Rhoda's boss, a self-avowed "chauvinistic pig," justified bypassing Rhoda on the ground that she had little knowledge of marketing loans to investors, and further, she was not familiar with the company's far-flung investors.

Realizing this, Rhoda launched an intense campaign to familiarize herself with some of the key investors — if not in person, then by mail. This she did quite well (very well, in some cases). Rhoda also amassed quite a bit of information on how to market loans.

At the next directors' meeting, Rhoda asked for and got a brief spot on the program. During her presentation, she exhibited a real knowledge of the market, along with testimonial letters from investors wanting to do business with Rhoda herself. As a result of this presentation, Rhoda was elected to the directorate. Another victory for the underdog!

Developing extreme competency

Without a doubt, acquiring extreme competency in any given area can be one of the surest and most effective routes to psychic advantage over others — even when you're the proverbial underdog.

Using a third party

If you were a college football star being sought by the pros, would you try to negotiate the contract yourself or would you turn it over to an agent?

If you're going to negotiate for yourself, and hope to get the best available deal, you're going to have to be adept in several areas. First, you'll need to know the going rate for "super stars," not to mention the bargaining "mood" or needs of the club you're negotiating with. You'll need to know about the legal ramifications of the contract, and finally, you'll need to possess sharp negotiating skills to insure getting best results.

Why the pros use a third party

The celebrity who does *not* possess these virtues — and there's little doubt that most do not — will be a definite underdog in any contract negotiation.

This is why, in increasing numbers, celebrities are using agents — disinterested, objective third parties — in dealing with corporations and other powerful entities. The agent becomes the *equalizer*. And based on some of the astronomical salaries super stars are dragging down these days, the third parties are getting results. In other words, they are definitely gaining psychic advantage for their clients.

What if you're not a super star?

"Fine," you might say, "but I'm not a super star. So what does all this mean to me?" It's a valid question. What does this mean to a typical management or professional person buried somewhere deep down in the organization?

Well, let's take a look at how Jack Baxter, personnel manager for Consolidated Homes, uses the technique. Jack is in a staff capacity, and as such is "subservient" to most line jobs.

Jack has most certainly an underdog role in dealing with most top-level people in line organizations. For example, Jack recently was faced with the problem of trying to "sell" the director of sales, Ralph LaPlante, on the idea of hiring some people who had previous sales experience in general real estate. The current policy precluded this possibility.

Why didn't the company hire former real estate salespeople? "We'd rather not have them," Ralph said. "We feel that if they had been successful salespeople in general real estate, they'd still be there. Besides, selling new homes is an entirely different bag.

"You see, our policy is to take people who have had some success in general selling and to teach them how to sell new homes. I might add that our policy seems to have worked quite well."

Jack had to concede that Ralph had what appeared to be a point. But he still felt strongly that the company was missing a good bet by totally excluding applicants just because they had had previous real estate experience.

Turning to a third party for leverage

He also was pragmatic enough to realize that for him to try to convince Ralph of this fact would be futile. In such a discussion, Ralph would have a decided psychic advantage for two reasons: First, he outranked him; second, Ralph spoke from sales experience while Jack did not. Jack realized that these facts put him in a pronounced underdog role, thus minimizing his chances of "winning" a confrontation.

At this point, Jack immediately sought an equalizer in the form of a knowledgeable "agent" — a strategy he had used successfully many times before.

This agent would have to meet several general requirements. He would have to have first-hand knowledge of the subject. He would have to be an "equal," or at least someone who had Ralph's confidence, and he would have to be someone who would *appear* to be completely detached from the issue.

After much thought, Jack came up with what appeared to be an ideal third-party equalizer.

Dusty Roberts gets the nod

He was Dusty Roberts, a former company salesman who had moved into management as assistant to the president. Though he was in a staff position, he carried weight because of his association with the president. And he was further highly regarded by Ralph because of his sales background.

Jack immediately launched his subtle campaign to convince Dusty that the company was passing up some "good bets" by totally excluding people with any real estate sales experience. After selling Dusty on this idea, he then sold him on the notion that he was just about the only one in the company who could convince Ralph of this point — and please, would he just give it a try?

An ego trip for Dusty

Flattered that he was being asked to use his influence, Dusty did just that. Within two weeks, he had sold Ralph on the idea of accepting a limited number of former real estate people if they met certain qualifications.

And so, another "win" for the underdog, who did it all, in this case, through an effective third party.

Next time you enter a transaction as the underdog and you just don't feel up to the task, look for a qualified third party. If you pick the right one, you can definitely gain psychic advantage.

Too modest — inarticulate

The equalizer strategy can be especially helpful to individuals who are too modest to champion their own cause, or who feel they are not articulate enough to tout their own capabilities. A couple of brief case histories illustrate the point.

Jack Wilson is a regional training director for an interstate manufacturing firm. As such, he stages seminars for management and executive personnel at the various divisions.

Jack says "not bad"

"How did the seminars go?" Jack's superiors at the home office inquire after Jack returns from a road trip. "Not bad," Jack replies modestly. "I ran into a few problems here and there, but on the whole — not bad at all."

Actually, the sessions went exceptionally well. Jack, you see, is afflicted with a severe case of *modesty*. Why? Who can say? And besides, the reason is somewhat beside the point.

Doesn't give a true picture

What *is* relevant is that management interprets Jack's "not bad" appraisal to mean "average," or even "lackluster," depending on the esteem in which they hold Jack. This reaction obviously nullifies Jack's chances to gain any degree of psychic advantage, since he is regarded as an "average trainer."

To gain a high psychic advantage with his superiors, Jack needs to either be less modest or use a third-party equalizer to state his case in less modest terms. The latter course is normally easier to follow, and it is the path Jack took.

Seeking a third-party opinion

Jack was reasonably confident that his programs were well received. Thus, after each session, he would ask the brightest and highest ranking members of the class to write their opinions of the seminar to the home office.

A fairly large percentage of those who were requested to write letters did so, and usually in glowing terms. Thus, instead of "not bad," the seminar appraisals became "excellent," "motivating," "extremely well conducted," "super," and so forth.

Thus, Jack was able to attain a much higher degree of psychic advantage through third parties, or *equalizers*, than he was by himself.

Aid for the verbally inadequate

This same principle might hold true for an individual who, though *willing* to tout his own capabilities, is not "verbal" enough to adequately articulate his thoughts.

John Septien, an accountant for an oil firm, has such a problem. The problem was magnified when John wanted to apply for a top job with another firm. It was a job for which he was admirably suited. But then there was the verbal communication problem.

Tries unique approach

John resolved the dilemma in a most unusual way. He got both present and past employers to "tape" their opinions of his performance in key-result areas.

He then carefully edited the tapes, down to a tight, interesting 10-minute presentation. At the interview, after a few introductory remarks, he played the tapes. They had the desired effect, and he got the job.

KEY IDEAS

We're all "underdogs" at one time or another, mainly because there are infinitely more "chiefs" than "Indians."

Under these circumstances, gaining psychic advantage is difficult, to say the least. But it *can* be done by:

- *Using the 4-P approach*
  - Learn to use pride, praise, preparation, and professionalism to the greatest advantage.
- *Acting with supreme confidence*
  - Act "as if" you were successful.
  - Don't be subservient to others.
  - Don't listen "too well."
  - Don't hang on to others' comments.
  - Learn to "talk tough."
- *Developing equalizers*
  - Assume extreme competence.
  - Exploit the third party to your advantage.

12

Using Psychic Advantage to Get Ahead in Business

You don't *have* to stand out in a crowd to get ahead in business and industry. But it can help, especially if you're just another face in the corporate crowd.

Throughout this book, we've discussed a number of tactics and strategies used by a wide range of business and professional people to gain psychic advantage. In this chapter, we'll discuss a few additional techniques aimed at enhancing your ability to get:

- Greater pay
- More promotions
- Added prestige

You can reap these benefits, and more, by:

- Raising your visibility level
- Establishing a strong identity
- Developing "political" savvy

Raising your visibility level

Who's going to notice you if you're just another number in a huge engineering drafting room or one of scores of young accountants wearing pin-striped suits in "accounts payable" or a junior executive joining the ranks of just about any big corporation anywhere?

The answer is painfully obvious: Probably no one... unless *you* make it happen! This is really what psychic advantage is all about.

Basically, the idea is to emulate the proven tactics and strategies that have worked for others and that can work well for you, assuming they fit your style and personality. The objective is to climb from obscurity to a position of relative importance in your organization.

Becoming a "publicity hound"

Quickly now, besides the top executive in your company, who are the best known people in the organization? That's right, people whose names — and pictures — appear most frequently in the company or outside publications. In other words, the people who routinely get the most publicity.

And how do the "publicity hounds" do it? By studying newspapers and trade journals to see what constitutes news and then cultivating the friendship of media types — editors, public relations directors, advertising managers, and the like.

Bob Newsome, manager of industrial relations for a large manufacturing firm, is a case in point. His name appears in the company newspaper no less than two dozen times a year, and in many cases, it is accompanied by a photograph. Here's how he does it.

How Bob gets publicity

Bob's first step is to get on a first-name basis with the company editor and public relations director. By this time, he is able to tell pretty well what likely will pass as a news story, so he gets on the phone and says, "Joe, I think I've got a little story for you." Joe usually responds favorably, since he has learned to trust Bob's judgment in such matters.

Here are just a few of the occasions in which Joe's name — and frequently his picture — appeared in the company or downtown newspaper. They are cited to give you a feel for how to become your own newshound.

Bob's in the news

- Bob was pictured presenting a check to one of his employees who had submitted a money-saving suggestion (all this at Bob's suggestion, of course).
- He was pictured presenting the annual safety award to the department with the best record. (The big boss was gone, so public relations asked Bob to substitute.)
- He was pictured receiving a plaque from the president of the United Fund for the company's participation. (Why was Bob in the picture? Because he suggested the story in the first place.)
- He was pictured cutting the ribbon at the opening of the company's new recreation area. (Bob was on the committee.)

The list goes on

- He was pictured congratulating the manager of manufacturing as the company's 500,000th product rolled off the assembly line.
- He was pictured with a 250-pound Marlin caught in an "epic struggle" off the Gulf of Mexico.
- He was pictured crowning the company's entry in the citywide "Miss Flame" contest, a photo that also made the downtown dailies.

Significantly, each of these and other photos to appear in print represented a legitimate news story, at least within the business community. And while Bob called public relations' attention to most of the stories, the publicity people knew Bob well enough to occasionally call on him. When you reach this point, you're a bona fide newshound.

And that's only the tip of the iceberg. Bob was quoted in innumerable instances on stories about safety, training, insurance, employment, and the gamut of activities under his supervision.

How a feature story helped

Perhaps the feature story that helped Bob's case most was the one about his winning the "Boss of the Year" honor. The story carried many interesting facts about Bob, including the one that claimed he had earned a Master's Degree from the Harvard Business School.

Actually, Bob dropped out of college during his junior year at a small college in the Midwest. But somewhere along the line, the "background information" on Bob in public relations had gotten slightly "altered."

The thrust of all this is that the publicity made Bob a celebrity of sorts in his own company. His name came up so frequently that when a list of names was drawn up for a new vice president, his came up, too. And not surprisingly, it was selected.

Learning the ropes

Undoubtedly, favorable publicity can give you a big boost in your quest for psychic advantage. Perhaps nothing else can do it quite as fast.

And the beauty of it is, you can gain the expertise a newshound needs without extensive formal study. You simply need to study newspapers and other publications to see what kind of material they use and then cultivate members of the press and the public relations department, and you're off and running. It can pay huge dividends.

Write and speak your way to psychic advantage

A manager is supposed to be an effective communicator. He or she should be able to write and speak well, and there's one sure-fire way to prove it. Do it!

Two of the surest ways to gain psychic advantage over your peers in the scramble for pay and promotion is to 1) write a "relevant" article for a generally accepted trade publication and 2) give a speech on almost anything.

Jerry Knight gets promotion

For example, Jerry Knight was elevated from associate engineer to group engineer in an unprecedented span of about four years. His performance was good enough, all right, but perhaps no better than that of many of his peers. Consensus is that Jerry's promotions were linked quite clearly to an article he wrote for a major trade publication.

The article surveyed the overall status of the nation's supersonic transport program, which was in its controversial infancy at the time. In the article, Jerry suggested converting one of his company's main products — a four-engine supersonic bomber — into a prototype supersonic transport, which could then demonstrate the feasibility of a twice-the-speed-of-sound airliner.

Catching the president's eye

The program never came about, but that is beside the point. What was important was that the article created lots of talk in the industry. And more importantly, it was seen and talked about by top management in Jerry's company — including the president. *Not* coincidentally, the first of Jerry's several promotions came about six months after the article appeared.

How do you find an appropriate subject for such an article? First, by looking around your company for a subject that's interesting or controversial and then simply writing about it. Second, by *studying* trade publications to see what kind of stuff they use and then querying the editor to see if he would be interested in your article. Most publications are almost always on the lookout for good material.

A book is even better

Writing a book about some aspect of your business or profession can, of course, be an even more rewarding experience. This point is perhaps best exemplified in the academic world, where professors must be published in order to move up in the institution.

Turning out a book is usually even more important to the business or professional person, since this sort of effort is made less frequently in the business world.

Thus people like Don Caruth, a Dallas management consultant, gains psychic advantage as author or co-author of over a dozen different books in the management field.

A speech is even better

A speech, depending on *how* and *to whom* it is given, can have even more dramatic results. The first step is to develop your speaking skills. One of the best ways to do this is to join a Toastmaster's group in your company or in your city. They're located nationwide.

The next step is to develop a speech or seminar in the area of your expertise and to get yourself "booked."

Talking your way up

I know of one such person, now a top executive in his company, who followed this pattern precisely. And there is absolutely no doubt in my mind that his oratorical prowess carried him to the top of the managerial ladder.

This executive's specialty is value engineering, a method used widely in industry today to keep costs down and quality up.

After getting his speaking skills up to speed (and he did, indeed, become a dynamic speaker), this executive developed a half-day seminar on the subject and presented it in his own plant.

Getting national acclaim

Later, he started doing the program for the special courses division of a local university. As a result of these activities, he soon was in demand as a speaker on the subject nationwide.

True, not everyone can become an accomplished platform speaker. But with practice, almost anyone can do well. It is an excellent, perhaps the best, way to gain a high degree of psychic advantage in your organization.

How to become an idea man

Very often, the person who gets the biggest raise or the fastest promotion is the "idea man" (or, of course, woman).

Fred Drake, a production manager, probably reached the top spot in his department because he was smart, capable, and industrious.

But so were a goodly number of his peers. No question about it, Fred gained psychic advantage early in his career with his company by developing a reputation as an "idea man."

How to gain immediate attention

Hardly a month went by that Fred did not submit a suggestion through the company's formalized suggestion program.

Some of his ideas were accepted; others were not. But the point is, Fred gained an almost instant reputation as a bright young man who was going places. What's more, he regularly received large annual "bonuses" in cash awards for his suggestions.

Other techniques

Not every company has such a formal program. In such cases, a person must obviously be more creative in establishing his reputation as an idea man.

Mike Bagley, a young accountant in a Big-8 firm, gained his reputation as an idea man simply by sending memos to departments in which he felt there was a cheaper or more effective way of doing business. Naturally, Mike's boss always got a carbon copy.

Establishing a strong identity

While gaining greater visibility in your organization, you might give considerable thought to establishing a strong and distinctive identity. Thought precedes action, and again, acting "as if" you are already in a dominant position tends to give you a degree of psychic advantage.

I've observed that many young — and many not-so-young — professionals are able to gain a rather surprising degree of psychic advantage by using the telephone effectively. For instance, let's take a look at how Jack Lambert, a would-be manager, does it.

Jack seems to consistently say and do the right things in his company. He also dresses for power, as discussed in a previous chapter.

Jack uses "phone power"

Here's how he often manages to gain psychic advantage with the telephone:

1. Jack *always* has his secretary place his calls, inside or outside of the company. By having his secretary call and say, "Will you hold a moment, Mr. Lambert is calling," Jack creates an aura of importance — at least to most people. This tends to put him one-up in the conversation before it really gets underway.

2. Jack has a reputation for talking loudly on the telephone, except, of course, when he doesn't want others to hear what he's saying. Otherwise, he'll boom his message ("Hell yes, I got seven new accounts in ten days," "I plan to close that deal next week," and so forth). His messages come through loud and clear, especially when the "right" people are around.

3. Jack makes a big deal out of incoming calls, too. He never answers the phone himself. Instead, he has his secretary answer, "Mr. Lambert is in an important meeting. May I have him call you, or is there anything I can help you with?" Or, if the call is "very important," Jack will have his secretary "interrupt" the meeting, again giving him a degree of psychic advantage going into the conversation.

Jack calls all this gaining psychic advantage through *telephone power.* There is little doubt that most of his associates identify him through his telephone techniques.

Gaining advantage through "status paper"

We talked about using status symbols as a means of gaining psychic advantage in a previous chapter. However, in this instance, we're talking about pieces of "paper" that people hang on the wall. It's another way to gain "instant" advantage and to establish a strong identity.

You would no doubt grasp the real significance of this

technique if you were to walk into the office of Lynn Turner, a Fort Worth management development consultant.

The walls of his rather spacious downtown office are lined almost solid with diplomas, certificates, pictures, and other mementoes of a long and colorful career.

Visitors are impressed

Visitors to the office are at first prone to listen to what Lynn is saying with only half a mind. The other half is busy scanning the "rogues gallery," taking in such items as: Master's Degree in Management Sciences, The University of Texas; President 1977 Rotary Club; President, Fort Worth School Board; President, Casa Manana Musicals; Director, TCU Ex-Letterman's Association; Outstanding Jaycee 1960, etc.

The pictures tell an interesting and even more dramatic story. Here's a photo of Lynn accepting an award from the mayor; another shows Lynn scoring the winning touchdown against Texas A&M (accompanied by a newspaper account of the game). Still another shows Lynn crowning "Miss Texas," plus many, many more.

Most visitors to Lynn's office react with predictable awe, giving him psychic advantage even before he utters a single word.

Naturally, it takes time and effort to assemble such symbols. But if you can, it is an effective way to "tell" people how great you are — to identify with you if you will — in the shortest possible time.

Developing a "contingency plan"

But Lynn is smart enough — and flexible enough — to realize that not everyone is impressed with such a blatant display of power. There are those who are "turned off" by such an ostentatious exhibit.

"It's easy to see when an unfavorable situation is developing," Lynn says. "And when it does, I simply say, 'Look, all this junk on the wall...I know it's gaudy as hell...but it's my wife's idea...and you know, I just did it to accommodate her.'" Such modesty is disarming and, except in extreme cases, casts Lynn as a "good guy" rather than a braggart.

Gaining identity as an expert

Another way to gain identity, and in turn psychic advantage, is to become an "expert" in some field or subject. Most often, the degree of psychic advantage you gain will be in direct proportion to the "remoteness" of the subject.

In other words, the less most others know about the subject, the more likely you are to be able to dazzle them with your brilliance. Frequently, a "new" subject will afford the greatest opportunity for you to gain psychic advantage.

Russell Long, a middle manager, is somewhat of an expert at becoming an *instant expert*. He does so mainly by staying on top of trends and innovations in several fields.

Dropping a new term

For example, at a recent management meeting, the group was discussing conventional lines of authority in an organization. When the unity-of-command principle was brought up, Long interjected, "Well, yes, there's a great deal to say about this relationship, but in a decentralized system such as ours, I really believe the *Matrix System* is much more applicable."

"The *what* system?" conferees say almost in unison.

"Matrix," Long responds, sensing that the group is unfamiliar with the term. "Well, it's a system that cuts across conventional lines of authority.

"Under the system, you can actually report to two or more bosses in key-result areas. You see…" and off he goes on a profound discussion. It's "profound" because he's got a monopoly, for the moment, on what it's all about.

Again, the "rules" of the game are simple. You ferret out a field or subject that's not too well known, bone up on the subject, and impart this information at the next business meeting, bridge club, or what have you. In time, you will become regarded as *profound*. And at this point, you naturally will have gained a pretty high degree of psychic advantage.

Developing political savvy

I would be remiss in not mentioning one of the most effective psychic advantage tools of all — plain old playing up to the boss. Playing office politics is still one of the surest ways to gain psychic advantage in the business world.

Actually, little more needs to be said about the games that are played in and out of offices everywhere. The basic idea is to find out what the boss likes to do, or what his tastes are, and to map your strategy accordingly.

Becoming a good golfer

This strategy seems to work especially well where the boss is an avid golf buff. Bob Foster illustrated the point shortly after he went to work for the director of an international electronics firm. Up to this point, Bob had been a "fun golfer." Now he took the game up in earnest, finally getting to the point where he could compete with his boss. Fully realizing that the idea is to compete and *not* defeat, Bob worked his way into the boss's foursome, first as a substitute and then as a regular.

Not too coincidentally, Bob was promoted to group supervisor within the year.

Politicking your way to a raise

Some contend that in the perennial battle for corporate bucks, the "squeaking wheel" is the one that gets greased. In other words, the person who persists in asking for a raise is the one who gets it.

Certainly there is some justification for this way of thinking. Squeaking wheels do often get greased; but by the same token they often get "derailed." It all depends on the nature and leadership style of your boss.

Duncan Todd's method

On the other hand, there are those who don't believe in squeaking at all; they believe in appropriate *action*. Duncan Todd has used the plan with some success in five different companies.

The appropriate time, he contends, is shortly before a performance review — a standard ritual in business in which the boss appraises the subordinate's performance for the previous six- or twelve-month period. The "action" should be something outstanding.

"Typically," Duncan said, "I manage to do something rather unusual two to three weeks before my review is due.

Puts in long hours

"One year, for example, I worked overtime — from 12 to 15 hours a day — for two solid weeks before the review. Another time, when I was in sales, I hit the ball real hard for about a full month. On still another occasion, I turned out a huge report exactly one week before my review was to come up.

"In each instance, I got a good raise. I might have gotten one anyway. But I'm convinced in my own mind that this stepped-up activity at the right time helped my cause considerably."

The "law of recency" at work

What Duncan really had working for himself was what psychologists call the law of recency: We tend to remember those things that happened most recently rather than those that happened several months before.

The logical conclusion: Bosses tend to remember — and reward — an employee's most *recent* contribution. It's a good point to keep in mind when you're getting ready for that annual salary review.

How to gain by "threat of loss"

There is another psychological principle — the *threat of loss* — that can be used to negotiate a raise. You've undoubtedly had a salesman pull it on you many times: "If you don't buy it today, it might be gone tomorrow."

Your first inclination is probably to say under your breath, "Yeah, I've heard this song before," and go about your business. But a *skilled* salesman can create a *legitimate* sense of urgency that can cause you to buy.

How Susan Phillips does it

Similarly, Susan Phillips, a high-powered ad account executive, can — and does — use the principle in wresting sizable salary increases from her fiscally conservative boss.

"I've been offered another job," Susan tells her boss at a propitious moment.

"More money?" the concerned boss inquires.

"Yes, I'm afraid so."

"How much more?"

"Oh, about a hundred a month."

"We can match it."

"I had hoped you would say that, cause I really want to stay with you."

When the boss says no

The threat works this time. But what if it had backfired? What if the boss had said no and wished her good luck?

Truth is, this is a high-stakes "game," one you should probably play only if you have the track record and temperament to carry it out. Or, if you have another job lined up.

The more subtle approach

For the less confident, Susan suggests some slightly more subtle approaches.

"I have found," she says, "that most bosses are notoriously nosy. They'll rifle your drawers, search your file cabinet, and take any opportunity they can to pry into your private business."

This gives you a wonderful chance to exploit the boss's curious nature. One way is to simply write down on your memo pad something like, "Call Al 245-9311. Urgent!"

The boss can't resist calling the number. The voice at the other end answers, "Acme Employment Service." And thus the seed has been planted.

Exercise with care

Again, these and other techniques aimed at giving you psychic advantage in getting a raise or promotion must be exercised with extreme care.

First, you must be confident of your own ability and reasonably sure your performance has been adequate. Second, you must be able to guess how your boss is likely to react to these tactics.

Remember, the squeaking wheel can get a raise or cause a breakdown.

KEY IDEAS

Can you use psychic advantage to get ahead in the hurly-burly world of business?

You can if you will take the time and effort to develop the sound strategies used by business and professional people. These include:

- *Raising your visibility level*
  - Become a "publicity hound."
  - Write your way to psychic advantage.
  - Talk your way to psychic advantage.
  - Become an "idea man."

- *Establishing a strong identity*
  - Use "telephone power."
  - Collect status papers.
  - Gain identity as an expert.

- *Developing political savvy*
  - Cultivate your boss.
  - Be a "squeaking wheel."
  - Take appropriate action.
  - Use "threat of loss."

Index

281